初學英文者該背什麼單字呢？根據教育部公佈的「最基本一千兩百字詞」，所有初學英語的中小學生的課本及課外補充教材，均將以這一千兩百字為標準，熟背這一千兩百字是學習英語的第一步，不論閱讀什麼教材，都會很輕鬆。

本書每個單字均附有音標、中文註釋及例句，版面特殊設計，同學背起來容易。英文例句沒有中文翻譯，有兩個理由，一是為版面美觀，每一頁都使同學感覺很輕鬆；二是為了老師授課方便，一天教二十個單字，兩個月就可以將這一千兩百個單字教完，並完成複習。

全書每 6 頁附有一回「自我測驗」，同學可以複習自己所背的單字，驗收成果。

「國中教育會考英語科」就是以這一千兩百字為命題範圍，為了應付「國中教育會考」，除了本書之外，本公司另編有「國中會考英語聽力測驗」和「國中會考英語模擬試題」，同學在背完這一千兩百字後，應乘勝追擊，利用這兩本書來加強自己的英文實力。

劉 毅

A a

用手機掃瞄聽錄音

a 〔ə,e〕 *art.* 一個
　Mary has *a* brother and *a* sister.

a few *adj.* 一些
　There are *a few* books on the table.

a little *adj.* 一些
　There is *a little* milk in the glass.

a lot *adv.* 很多
　You've changed *a lot*.

able 〔'ebḷ〕 *adj.* 能夠的
　Nick is not *able* to come to the party.

about 〔ə'baʊt〕 *prep.* 關於
　This book is *about* cars.

above 〔ə'bʌv〕 *prep.* 在…上面
　The kite is flying *above* the tree.

abroad 〔ə'brɔd〕 *adv.* 在國外
　Have you ever traveled *abroad*?

across 〔ə'krɔs〕 *prep.* 橫越
　I walked *across* the road.

act 〔 ækt 〕 *n.* 行為
No *act* of kindness is ever wasted.

action 〔 'ækʃən 〕 *n.* 行動
Actions speak louder than words.

actor 〔 'æktə 〕 *n.* 演員
He is a famous film *actor*.

actress 〔 'æktrɪs 〕 *n.* 女演員
Sarah wants to be an *actress*.

afraid 〔 ə'fred 〕 *adj.* 害怕的
Don't be *afraid* of my puppy.

after 〔 'æftə 〕 *prep.* 在…之後
Monday comes *after* Sunday.

afternoon 〔 ‚æftə'nun 〕 *n.* 下午
My father jogs every *afternoon*.

again 〔 ə'gɛn 〕 *adv.* 再一次
Jim has read that book but he is reading it *again*.

age 〔 edʒ 〕 *n.* 年齡
What's the *age* of that old building?

ago 〔 ə'go 〕 *adv.* 以前
I went to France about two years *ago*.

agree 〔 ə'gri 〕 *v.* 同意
We all *agree* with you.

ahead 〔 ə'hɛd 〕 *adv.* 在前方
John ran *ahead* of the other boys.

air 〔 ɛr 〕 *n.* 空氣
I need some fresh *air*.

airplane 〔'ɛr͵plen 〕 *n.* 飛機 (= *plane*)
He took a trip by *airplane*.

airport 〔'ɛr͵port 〕 *n.* 機場
An *airport* is a busy place.

all 〔 ɔl 〕 *adj.* 全部的
Sally read *all* the books.

almost 〔'ɔl͵most 〕 *adv.* 幾乎
Dinner is *almost* ready.

along 〔 ə'lɔŋ 〕 *prep.* 沿著
Cathy is walking *along* the street with her mother.

already 〔 ɔl'rɛdɪ 〕 *adv.* 已經
She has *already* finished her homework.

also 〔'ɔlso 〕 *adv.* 也
He is kind and *also* honest.

although 〔 ɔl'ðo 〕 *conj.* 雖然
Although it was raining, Joan still wanted to go out.

always 〔'ɔlwez 〕 *adv.* 總是
The bus *always* comes at seven.

a.m. 〔'e'ɛm 〕 *adv.* 上午
I will meet you at 8:15 *a.m.*

am 〔 æm 〕 *v.* 是【be 的第一人稱】
I *am* an outgoing person.

America 〔 ə'mɛrɪkə 〕 *n.* 美國 (= *the U.S.A.*)
She moved to *America* two years ago.

American 〔 ə'mɛrɪkən 〕 *n.* 美國人
There are two *Americans* in her class.

an 〔 æn 〕 *art.* 一個
Which is bigger, *an* orange or *an* egg?

and 〔 ænd 〕 *conj.* 和

The children sang *and* danced at the party.

angry 〔'æŋgrɪ 〕 *adj.* 生氣的

Mother was *angry* when John cried.

animal 〔'ænəml̩ 〕 *n.* 動物

There are many *animals* in the zoo.

another 〔 ə'nʌðɚ 〕 *adj.* 另一個

The shirt is too small; I need *another* one.

answer 〔'ænsɚ 〕 *v.* 回答

The question is so difficult that we can't *answer* it.

ant 〔 ænt 〕 *n.* 螞蟻

An *ant* is a small insect.

any 〔'ɛnɪ 〕 *adj.* 任何的

There isn't *any* sugar in the jar.

anybody 〔'ɛnɪˌbɑdɪ 〕 *pron.* 任何人

Did he leave a message for *anybody*?

anyone 〔'ɛnɪˌwʌn 〕 *pron.* 任何人

If *anyone* calls, tell him I'll be back at five.

anything (ˈɛnɪˌθɪŋ) *pron.* 任何東西
Is there *anything* in your bag?

apartment (əˈpɑrtmənt) *n.* 公寓
Ben and his sister lived in an *apartment*.

appear (əˈpɪr) *v.* 出現
A rainbow always *appears* after the rain.

apple (ˈæpl̩) *n.* 蘋果
An *apple* a day keeps the doctor away.

April (ˈeprəl) *n.* 四月
April is the fourth month of the year.

are (ɑr) *v.* 是【be 的第二人稱與各人稱的複數】
Cindy and Lucy *are* good friends.

arm (ɑrm) *n.* 手臂
She carries her son in her *arms*.

around (əˈraʊnd) *prep.* 環繞
He walked *around* the park three times.

arrive (əˈraɪv) *v.* 到達
The Dalai Lama will *arrive* here on Monday.

art (ɑrt) *n.* 藝術
She teaches *art* history.

自我測驗

- [ ] able　　　　_____
- [ ] abroad　　　_____
- [ ] act　　　　　_____
- [ ] afraid　　　 _____
- [ ] agree　　　　_____

- [ ] airplane　　 _____
- [ ] along　　　　_____
- [ ] already　　　_____
- [ ] angry　　　　_____
- [ ] another　　　_____

- [ ] ant　　　　　_____
- [ ] apple　　　　_____
- [ ] arm　　　　　_____
- [ ] around　　　 _____
- [ ] art　　　　　_____

Check List

1.	關　於	a	_about_	t
2.	橫　越	a	_____	s
3.	行　動	a	_____	n
4.	演　員	a	_____	r
5.	空　氣	a	_____	r
6.	機　場	a	_____	t
7.	幾　乎	a	_____	t
8.	雖　然	a	_____	h
9.	動　物	a	_____	l
10.	回　答	a	_____	r
11.	任何的	a	_____	y
12.	公　寓	a	_____	t
13.	出　現	a	_____	r
14.	四　月	A	_____	l
15.	到　達	a	_____	e

as〔æz〕*prep.* 作為

It can be used *as* a knife.

ask〔æsk〕*v.* 問

She *asked* me how to get there.

at〔æt〕*prep.* 在…

There is someone *at* the door.

attack〔əˈtæk〕*v.* 攻擊

The tiger *attacked* and killed a deer for food.

August〔ˈɔgəst〕*n.* 八月

August is the eighth month of the year.

aunt〔ænt〕*n.* 阿姨

My *aunt* is coming to see us.

autumn〔ˈɔtəm〕*n.* 秋天（= *fall*）

Autumn is the season between summer and winter.

away〔əˈwe〕*adv.* 離開

They're *away* on holiday.

B b

baby〔ˈbebɪ〕*n.* 嬰兒

Both the mother and the *baby* are doing well.

back ﹝ bæk ﹞ *n.* 背面
The price is on the *back* of the book.

bad ﹝ bæd ﹞ *adj.* 不好的
The weather was really *bad*.

badminton ﹝'bædmɪntən﹞ *n.* 羽毛球
Badminton is a very interesting sport.

bag ﹝ bæg ﹞ *n.* 袋子
Tom carried a *bag* to school.

bake ﹝ bek ﹞ *v.* 烘烤
I like to *bake* cakes from time to time.

bakery ﹝'bekərɪ﹞ *n.* 麵包店
There is a very good *bakery* near my house.

balcony ﹝'bælkənɪ﹞ *n.* 陽台；包廂
You can see the ocean from our *balcony*.

ball ﹝ bɔl ﹞ *n.* 球
We need a *ball* to play basketball.

banana ﹝ bə'nænə ﹞ *n.* 香蕉
Monkeys like to eat *bananas*.

band ﹝ bænd ﹞ *n.* 樂隊
The *band* is playing.

bank〔 bæŋk 〕*n.* 銀行
Albert puts his money in the *bank*.

barbecue〔'bɑrbɪ͵kju 〕*n.* 烤肉
We'll have a *barbecue* this Friday.

base〔 bes 〕*n.* 基礎；基地
He used Stephen King's novel as the *base* of his movie.

baseball〔'bes͵bɔl 〕*n.* 棒球
Baseball is very popular in America.

basket〔'bæskɪt 〕*n.* 籃子
This *basket* is made of bamboo.

basketball〔'bæskɪt͵bɔl 〕*n.* 籃球
We play *basketball* every day.

bat〔 bæt 〕*n.* 球棒；蝙蝠
Ben used a *bat* to hit the ball in the game.

bath〔 bæθ 〕*n.* 洗澡
Sue took a *bath* because she was dirty.

bathroom〔'bæθ͵rum 〕*n.* 浴室
She went into the *bathroom* and took a shower.

be 〔 bi 〕 *v.* 是；成爲

I want to *be* a teacher.

beach 〔 bitʃ 〕 *n.* 海灘

John likes to go to the *beach*.

bean 〔 bin 〕 *n.* 豆子

A *bean* is a vegetable.

bear 〔 bɛr 〕 *n.* 熊

A *bear* is a wild animal.

beautiful 〔'bjutəfəl 〕 *adj.* 美麗的

The flowers in the garden look so *beautiful*.

because 〔 bɪ'kɔz 〕 *conj.* 因爲

Linda was late *because* it was raining.

become 〔 bɪ'kʌm 〕 *v.* 變成

They *became* good friends at once.

bed 〔 bɛd 〕 *n.* 床

I fell off my *bed* last night.

bedroom 〔'bɛd,rum 〕 *n.* 臥室

I have my own *bedroom*.

bee 〔 bi 〕 *n.* 蜜蜂

A *bee* is an insect which makes honey.

beef〔 bif 〕*n.* 牛肉
You can buy *beef* from a butcher.

been〔 bɪn 〕*v.* 是【be 的過去分詞】
He has *been* a teacher since 1990.

before〔 bɪˈfor 〕*conj.* 在…之前
You must wash your hands *before* you eat.

begin〔 bɪˈgɪn 〕*v.* 開始
School *begins* at eight in the morning.

behind〔 bɪˈhaɪnd 〕*prep.* 在…後面
The playground is *behind* our school.

believe〔 bɪˈliv 〕*v.* 相信
Do you *believe* in magic?

bell〔 bɛl 〕*n.* 鐘
I can hear the church *bell* ringing.

belong〔 bəˈlɔŋ 〕*v.* 屬於
This book *belongs* to me.

below〔 bəˈlo 〕*prep.* 在…以下
Students who have marks *below* 60 will have
to take the exam again.

belt〔bɛlt〕*n.* 皮帶
Rose gave a *belt* to her father on his birthday.

bench〔bɛntʃ〕*n.* 長椅
The man has been sitting on the *bench* all day long.

beside〔bɪˈsaɪd〕*prep.* 在…旁邊
Pat and Paul sat *beside* each other in class.

between〔bɪˈtwin〕*prep.* 在（兩者）之間
The boy is standing *between* two trees.

bicycle〔ˈbaɪsɪkl̩〕*n.* 腳踏車（＝*bike*）
Do you know who stole the *bicycle*?

big〔bɪg〕*adj.* 大的
An elephant is a *big* animal.

bird〔bɝd〕*n.* 鳥
Most *birds* can fly.

birthday〔ˈbɝθˌde〕*n.* 生日
For her *birthday* I bought her a doll.

bite〔baɪt〕*v.* 咬
My puppy always *bites* my shoes.

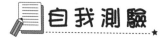

自我測驗

- ☐ ask _____
- ☐ attack _____
- ☐ aunt _____
- ☐ back _____
- ☐ bakery _____

- ☐ balcony _____
- ☐ barbecue _____
- ☐ baseball _____
- ☐ bean _____
- ☐ become _____

- ☐ behind _____
- ☐ belong _____
- ☐ belt _____
- ☐ between _____
- ☐ bite _____

 **Check List**

1.	八　月	A	*August*	t
2.	秋　天	a		n
3.	離　開	a		y
4.	不好的	b		d
5.	羽毛球	b		n
6.	烘　烤	b		e
7.	樂　隊	b		d
8.	基　礎	b		e
9.	球　棒	b		t
10.	熊	b		r
11.	臥　室	b		m
12.	開　始	b		n
13.	相　信	b		e
14.	長　椅	b		h
15.	腳踏車	b		e

black ﹝ blæk ﹞ *adj.* 黑色的
Sue's hair is *black*.

blackboard ﹝'blæk‚bord ﹞ *n.* 黑板
The teacher writes a sentence on the
blackboard.

blanket ﹝'blæŋkɪt ﹞ *n.* 毯子
The baby is covered with the *blanket*.

blind ﹝ blaɪnd ﹞ *adj.* 盲的
Blind children have to go to special schools.

block ﹝ blɑk ﹞ *n.* 街區
The store is three *blocks* away.

blow ﹝ blo ﹞ *v.* 吹
She *blows* her hair dry.

blue ﹝ blu ﹞ *adj.* 藍色的
Helen is wearing a *blue* dress.

boat ﹝ bot ﹞ *n.* 船
Tom and Dan are in a *boat*.

body ﹝'bɑdɪ ﹞ *n.* 身體
Eat right and you will have a healthy *body*.

boil 〔 bɔɪl 〕 *v.* 沸騰
The water is *boiling*.

book 〔 bʊk 〕 *n.* 書
Anna read a lot of *books* before the exam.

bookstore 〔'bʊk͵stor 〕 *n.* 書店
Tom is going to the *bookstore* to buy a book.

bored 〔 bord 〕 *adj.* 感到無聊的
The students were *bored* with the lesson.

boring 〔'borɪŋ 〕 *adj.* 無聊的
Martin feels that typing is a *boring* job.

born 〔 bɔrn 〕 *adj.* 出生的
The kitten was *born* yesterday.

borrow 〔'baro 〕 *v.* 借（入）
May I *borrow* your bicycle for a day?

boss 〔 bɔs 〕 *n.* 老闆
The new *boss* is very strict.

both 〔 boθ 〕 *pron.* 兩者都
Sharon and Mark *both* came to class late.

bottle 〔'batḷ 〕 *n.* 瓶子
Harry is pouring a drink from a *bottle*.

bottom (ˈbɑtəm) *n.* 底部
The ship sank to the *bottom* of the sea.

bow (baʊ) *v.* 鞠躬 *n.* 船首
The student *bowed* to his teacher.

bowl (bol) *n.* 碗
He has finished five *bowls* of rice.

box (bɑks) *n.* 盒子
Linda gave me a *box* of candies.

boy (bɔɪ) *n.* 男孩
Billy is a naughty *boy* who lives near my house.

bread (brɛd) *n.* 麵包
Bread is made from flour.

break (brek) *v.* 打破
Who *broke* the window?

breakfast (ˈbrɛkfəst) *n.* 早餐
We always have *breakfast* at 7:00 a.m.

bridge (brɪdʒ) *n.* 橋
There is a *bridge* across the river.

bright 〔 braɪt 〕 *adj.* 明亮的

The box was painted *bright* green.

bring 〔 brɪŋ 〕 *v.* 帶來

I *brought* the book you wanted.

brother 〔'brʌðɚ〕 *n.* 兄弟

These two boys are *brothers*.

brown 〔 braʊn 〕 *adj.* 棕色的

John likes to wear *brown* shoes.

brush 〔 brʌʃ 〕 *n.* 刷子

William uses a small *brush* to paint his house.

bug 〔 bʌg 〕 *n.* 小蟲   *v.* 竊聽

I hate *bugs*.

build 〔 bɪld 〕 *v.* 建造

They can *build* a house in one week.

bun 〔 bʌn 〕 *n.* 小圓麵包

Mary likes to eat *buns*.

burn 〔 bɝn 〕 *v.* 燃燒

In winter, people *burn* wood to keep warm.

bus 〔 bʌs 〕 *n.* 公車

Joan takes a *bus* to school every day.

business (ˈbɪznɪs) *n.* 生意
We didn't do much *business* with the company.

businessman (ˈbɪznɪsˌmæn) *n.* 商人
My father is a *businessman*.

busy (ˈbɪzɪ) *adj.* 忙碌的
My father is *busy* with his work.

but (bʌt) *conj.* 但是
She would like to go to the party *but* she can't.

butter (ˈbʌtɚ) *n.* 奶油
Mom put some *butter* in the corn soup.

butterfly (ˈbʌtɚˌflaɪ) *n.* 蝴蝶
A *butterfly* is an insect with wings full of bright colors.

buy (baɪ) *v.* 買
Tim went to the supermarket to *buy* food.

by (baɪ) *prep.* 搭乘
Mike goes to school *by* bus.

C c

cage 〔 kedʒ 〕 *n.* 籠子
There are two lions in the *cage*.

cake 〔 kek 〕 *n.* 蛋糕
Chocolate *cake* is my favorite dessert.

call 〔 kɔl 〕 *v.* 打電話給～
I will *call* my mother at her office.

camera 〔'kæmərə 〕 *n.* 照相機
Lisa used a *camera* to take pictures of her
friends.

camp 〔 kæmp 〕 *v.* 露營
We will *camp* in the park tonight.

can 〔 kæn 〕 *aux.* 能夠
Wendy *can* type 80 words per minute.

candle 〔'kændļ 〕 *n.* 蠟燭
Michelle has twelve *candles* on her birthday
cake.

candy 〔'kændɪ 〕 *n.* 糖果
You eat too much *candy*.

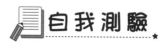

- ☐ blackboard _____
- ☐ blanket _____
- ☐ blow _____
- ☐ bored _____
- ☐ borrow _____

- ☐ bottle _____
- ☐ bow _____
- ☐ break _____
- ☐ bring _____
- ☐ bun _____

- ☐ business _____
- ☐ butter _____
- ☐ cage _____
- ☐ call _____
- ☐ camp _____

✎ Check List

1.	黑色的	b _____black_____	k
2.	盲　的	b _____	d
3.	沸　騰	b _____	l
4.	無聊的	b _____	g
5.	出生的	b _____	n
6.	老　闆	b _____	s
7.	底　部	b _____	m
8.	橋	b _____	e
9.	明亮的	b _____	t
10.	刷　子	b _____	h
11.	建　造	b _____	d
12.	燃　燒	b _____	n
13.	忙碌的	b _____	y
14.	照相機	c _____	a
15.	蠟　燭	c _____	e

cap 〔 kæp 〕 *n.* (無邊的) 帽子
Don't forget to wear a *cap* if you go out in the sun.

car 〔 kɑr 〕 *n.* 汽車
Tom drives an old *car*.

card 〔 kɑrd 〕 *n.* 卡片
Danny sent a Christmas *card* to me.

care 〔 kɛr 〕 *v.* 在乎
I don't *care* what happens.

careful 〔'kɛrfəl 〕 *adj.* 小心的
Be *careful* when you drive the car.

carry 〔'kærɪ 〕 *v.* 攜帶
Linda *carried* a big box.

case 〔 kes 〕 *n.* 情況
That's a very unusual *case*.

castle 〔'kæsl̩ 〕 *n.* 城堡
Long ago, kings lived in *castles*.

cat 〔 kæt 〕 *n.* 貓
Many people keep *cats* as pets.

catch 〔 kætʃ 〕 *v.* 捕捉
Jenny keeps a cat to *catch* mice.

celebrate 〔'sɛləˌbret 〕 *v.* 慶祝
We *celebrated* Judy's birthday yesterday.

cell phone *n.* 手機
We can talk on a *cell phone* at any time.

cent 〔 sɛnt 〕 *n.* 一分錢
There are 100 *cents* to a dollar.

center 〔'sɛntɚ 〕 *n.* 中心
New York is a *center* of trade.

centimeter 〔'sɛntəˌmitɚ 〕 *n.* 公分
There are 100 *centimeters* in one meter.

chair 〔 tʃɛr 〕 *n.* 椅子
I like to sit in a comfortable *chair* while
watching TV.

chalk 〔 tʃɔk 〕 *n.* 粉筆
My teacher is writing with a piece of *chalk*.

chance 〔 tʃæns 〕 *n.* 機會
At the party every child has a *chance* to win a
prize.

change ﹝ tʃendʒ ﹞ *v.* 改變
Adam *changes* his clothes before he goes to bed.

cheap ﹝ tʃip ﹞ *adj.* 便宜的
Everything is *cheap* at that supermarket.

cheat ﹝ tʃit ﹞ *v.* 欺騙
Kim was *cheated* by the stranger.

check ﹝ tʃɛk ﹞ *v.* 檢查
Please *check* the door before going to bed.

cheer ﹝ tʃɪr ﹞ *v.* 使高興
Going to a KTV after the exam will *cheer* me.

cheese ﹝ tʃiz ﹞ *n.* 乳酪;起司
I'm fond of French *cheese*.

chess ﹝ tʃɛs ﹞ *n.* 西洋棋
My young brother loves playing *chess*.

chicken ﹝ 'tʃɪkən ﹞ *n.* 雞肉;雞
I like to eat fried *chicken*.

child ﹝ tʃaɪld ﹞ *n.* 小孩
My aunt has only one *child*.

China ('tʃaɪnə) *n.* 中國
China is a big country.

Chinese (tʃaɪ'niz) *n.* 中國人
The *Chinese* are a friendly people.

chocolate ('tʃɔkəlɪt) *n.* 巧克力
My sister made a *chocolate* cake yesterday.

choose (tʃuz) *v.* 選擇
Sally has to *choose* the dress she likes the best.

chopsticks ('tʃɑp,stɪks) *n. pl.* 筷子
Most Asians eat with *chopsticks*.

Christmas ('krɪsməs) *n.* 聖誕節
Christmas is on the 25th of December.

church (tʃɜtʃ) *n.* 教堂
People go to *church* to pray.

circle ('sɜkḷ) *n.* 圓圈
Peter drew a *circle* in my book.

city ('sɪtɪ) *n.* 城市
Paris is the capital *city* of France.

clap (klæp) *v.* 鼓掌
Alice *clapped* when the music ended.

class 〔 klæs 〕 *n.* 班級
There are thirty students in our *class*.

classmate 〔 'klæs‚met 〕 *n.* 同班同學
Robbie and I have been *classmates* for two years.

classroom 〔 'klæs‚rum 〕 *n.* 教室
What are you doing in the *classroom*?

clean 〔 klin 〕 *adj.* 乾淨的
The air is not *clean* in big cities.

clear 〔 klır 〕 *adj.* 清楚的
He didn't give a *clear* explanation.

clerk 〔 klɜk 〕 *n.* 店員；職員
My mother works as a *clerk* in the shop.

climb 〔 klaım 〕 *v.* 爬
We will *climb* Mt. Jade this summer.

clock 〔 klɑk 〕 *n.* 鐘
I'm going to buy a new *clock* this weekend.

close 〔 kloz 〕 *v.* 關閉
He *closed* his store earlier than usual.

clothes 〔 kloðz 〕 *n.pl.* 衣服
We need cloth to make *clothes*.

cloudy 〔'klaʊdɪ 〕 *adj.* 多雲的
Today is a *cloudy* day.

club 〔 klʌb 〕 *n.* 俱樂部;社團
Jessica belongs to the drama *club*.

coat 〔 kot 〕 *n.* 外套
Everybody likes to wear a *coat* in the winter.

coffee 〔'kɔfɪ 〕 *n.* 咖啡
I like to drink *coffee* with milk.

Coke 〔 kok 〕 *n.* 可口可樂
I would like to have a *Coke*.

cold 〔 kold 〕 *adj.* 寒冷的
We had a *cold* winter.

collect 〔 kə'lɛkt 〕 *v.* 收集
Why do you *collect* dolls?

color 〔'kʌlɚ 〕 *n.* 顏色
My favorite *color* is blue.

comb 〔 kom 〕 *n.* 梳子
We use a *comb* to make our hair tidy.

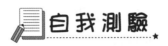
自我測驗

- [ ] car   _____
- [ ] careful   _____
- [ ] case   _____
- [ ] catch   _____
- [ ] cent   _____

- [ ] chalk   _____
- [ ] change   _____
- [ ] cheat   _____
- [ ] cheese   _____
- [ ] China   _____

- [ ] chopsticks   _____
- [ ] clap   _____
- [ ] clean   _____
- [ ] cloudy   _____
- [ ] color   _____

Check List

1. 在 乎	c	_care_	e
2. 攜 帶	c		y
3. 城 堡	c		e
4. 慶 祝	c		e
5. 公 分	c		r
6. 機 會	c		e
7. 便宜的	c		p
8. 檢 查	c		k
9. 使高興	c		r
10. 選 擇	c		e
11. 圓 圈	c		e
12. 清楚的	c		r
13. 爬	c		b
14. 收 集	c		t
15. 梳 子	c		b

come〔kʌm〕 *v.* 來
Mr. Brown *comes* to New York every summer.

comfortable〔'kʌmfətəbḷ〕 *adj.* 舒適的
This chair doesn't look *comfortable*.

comic〔'kɑmɪk〕 *adj.* 漫畫的
Ted loves reading *comic* books.

common〔'kɑmən〕 *adj.* 常見的
Smith is a very *common* last name in England.

computer〔kəm'pjutɚ〕 *n.* 電腦
Computers are necessary for everyone.

convenient〔kən'vinjənt〕 *adj.* 方便的
Is Friday *convenient* for you?

cook〔kʊk〕 *v.* 煮
Jennifer *cooked* noodles for lunch.

cookie〔'kʊkɪ〕 *n.* 餅乾
Sandra is good at making *cookies*.

cool〔kul〕 *adj.* 涼爽的
Please keep the medicine in a *cool* and dry
place.

copy ('kɑpɪ) *v.* 抄寫；影印
Copy down the questions in your notebook.

corner ('kɔrnɚ) *n.* 角落
The post office is right on the *corner*.

correct (kə'rɛkt) *adj.* 正確的
All the answers are *correct*.

cost (kɔst) *v.* 花費
How much will it *cost* to repair this car?

couch (kautʃ) *n.* 長沙發
There is a cat on the *couch*.

could (kud) *aux.* 能夠【can 的過去式】
I'm so glad you *could* come.

count (kaunt) *v.* 數
My little sister can *count* from 1 to 10.

country ('kʌntrɪ) *n.* 鄉下；國家
I prefer *country* life.

course (kɔrs) *n.* 課程
She took a *course* in French literature.

cousin ('kʌzn̩) *n.* 堂（表）兄弟姊妹
I have six *cousins* on my mother's side.

cover ('kʌvɚ) *v.* 覆蓋
The car is *covered* with snow.

cow (kaʊ) *n.* 母牛
You can see *cows* on the farm.

crazy ('krezɪ) *adj.* 發瘋的；狂熱的
She went *crazy* with fear.

cross (krɔs) *v.* 橫越
We *crossed* a lake in a boat.

cry (kraɪ) *v.* 哭
The little babies always *cry*.

cup (kʌp) *n.* 杯子
I broke my *cup* yesterday.

cut (kʌt) *v.* 切；割
She *cut* her finger with a knife.

cute (kjut) *adj.* 可愛的
She is such a *cute* girl.

D d

daddy ('dædɪ) *n.* 爸爸
Peter is those children's *daddy*.

dance 〔 dæns 〕 *v.* 跳舞
We can *dance* at the party tomorrow.

dangerous 〔'dendʒərəs〕 *adj.* 危險的
The river is *dangerous* to cross.

dark 〔 dɑrk 〕 *adj.* 黑暗的
The house is very *dark* at night.

date 〔 det 〕 *n.* 日期
What is your *date* of birth?

daughter 〔'dɔtɚ〕 *n.* 女兒
Lucy is the only *daughter* of the family.

day 〔 de 〕 *n.* 天；日子
What *day* is today?

dead 〔 dɛd 〕 *adj.* 死的
Susan found a *dead* cat in her house.

deal 〔 dil 〕 *v.* 處理
I spent the morning *dealing* with my e-mails.

dear 〔 dɪr 〕 *adj.* 親愛的
Alice is my *dear* friend.

December 〔 dɪ'sɛmbɚ〕 *n.* 十二月
December is the last month of the year.

decide ﹝dɪ'saɪd﹞ v. 決定
She has *decided* to marry him.

delicious ﹝dɪ'lɪʃəs﹞ adj. 美味的
What a *delicious* dinner we enjoyed tonight!

dentist ﹝'dɛntɪst﹞ n. 牙醫
John hates going to the *dentist's*.

department store n. 百貨公司
I'm on my way to the *department store*.

desk ﹝dɛsk﹞ n. 書桌
My grandfather made this *desk* for me.

dictionary ﹝'dɪkʃənˌɛrɪ﹞ n. 字典
Cindy looks up every word in the *dictionary*.

did ﹝dɪd﹞ aux. 做【do 的過去式】
Did you go to the party last night?

die ﹝daɪ﹞ v. 死
My grandmother *died* in 1998.

different ﹝'dɪfərənt﹞ adj. 不同的
A girl is *different* from a boy.

difficult ﹝'dɪfəˌkʌlt﹞ adj. 困難的
English is not too *difficult* to learn.

dig 〔 dɪg 〕 *v.* 挖
The gardener has to *dig* a hole to plant a tree.

dining room *n.* 飯廳
Have we got any coffee in the *dining room*?

dinner 〔'dɪnɚ 〕 *n.* 晚餐
I would like to eat noodles for *dinner*.

dirty 〔'dɝtɪ 〕 *adj.* 髒的
Allen washed all his *dirty* clothes last night.

dish 〔 dɪʃ 〕 *n.* 盤子
Used *dishes* are put in the sink.

do 〔 du 〕 *v.* 做
I *do* my homework every day.

doctor 〔'dɑktɚ 〕 *n.* 醫生 (= *Dr.*)
She went to see the *doctor* at two o'clock.

dodge ball *n.* 躲避球
We played *dodge ball* in the afternoon.

does 〔 dʌz 〕 *aux.* 做【do 的第三人稱】
What *does* he want to drink?

dog 〔 dɔg 〕 *n.* 狗
We keep two *dogs* at home.

自我測驗

- [ ] come _____
- [ ] comfortable _____
- [ ] corner _____
- [ ] correct _____
- [ ] cousin _____

- [ ] cross _____
- [ ] cut _____
- [ ] dark _____
- [ ] dead _____
- [ ] December _____

- [ ] dentist _____
- [ ] different _____
- [ ] dig _____
- [ ] dirty _____
- [ ] dish _____

Check List

1. 漫畫的　　c ___*comic*___ c
2. 常見的　　c _____ n
3. 方便的　　c _____ t
4. 花　費　　c _____ t
5. 數　　　　c _____ t

6. 覆　蓋　　c _____ r
7. 哭　　　　c _____ y
8. 跳　舞　　d _____ e
9. 危險的　　d _____ s
10. 處　理　　d _____ l

11. 決　定　　d _____ e
12. 美味的　　d _____ s
13. 字　典　　d _____ y
14. 困難的　　d _____ t
15. 醫　生　　d _____ r

doll 〔 dɑl 〕 *n.* 洋娃娃
Most girls like to play with *dolls*.

dollar 〔'dɑlɚ 〕 *n.* 元
One *dollar* is the same as 100 cents.

door 〔 dor 〕 *n.* 門
Please lock the *door* when you come in.

dot 〔 dɑt 〕 *n.* 點
Her skirt is green with red *dots*.

down 〔 daʊn 〕 *adv.* 向下
The old house has fallen *down*.

dozen 〔'dʌzn̩ 〕 *n.* 一打
Karen has a *dozen* roses.

Dr. 〔'dɑktɚ 〕 *n.* 博士；醫生
Dr. Lee is a very nice person.

dragon 〔'drægən 〕 *n.* 龍
In fairy tales, *dragons* are dangerous animals.

draw 〔 drɔ 〕 *v.* 畫
Amy is *drawing* a tree with a pencil.

drawer 〔 drɔr 〕 *n.* 抽屜
I put the book in the left-hand *drawer*.

dream ﹝ drim ﹞ *n.* 夢
Ben woke up because he had a bad *dream*.

dress ﹝ drɛs ﹞ *n.* 洋裝
Linda ironed her *dress* before wearing it.

drink ﹝ drɪŋk ﹞ *v.* 喝
I *drink* water when I am thirsty.

drive ﹝ draɪv ﹞ *v.* 開車
After working, Bob *drove* home.

driver ﹝ 'draɪvɚ ﹞ *n.* 駕駛人
Sam is a careful *driver*.

drop ﹝ drɑp ﹞ *v.* 掉落
The book *dropped* from the desk to the floor.

drum ﹝ drʌm ﹞ *n.* 鼓
Peter plays drums every day.

dry ﹝ draɪ ﹞ *adj.* 乾的
When Joan arrived, her umbrella was wet but
her clothes were *dry*.

duck ﹝ dʌk ﹞ *n.* 鴨子
Alice is feeding the *ducks* in the pond.

dumpling〔'dʌmplɪŋ〕*n.* 水餃

I ate *dumplings* for lunch today.

during〔'djʊrɪŋ〕*prep.* 在⋯期間

Albert always sleeps *during* class.

E e

each〔itʃ〕*adj.* 每一個

Each student in the class got a present.

ear〔ɪr〕*n.* 耳朵

We hear with our *ears*.

early〔'ɜlɪ〕*adv.* 早

Most students get up *early* in the morning.

earth〔ɜθ〕*n.* 地球

We live on the *earth*.

Easter〔'istɚ〕*n.* 復活節

The kids get two weeks off school at *Easter*.

east〔ist〕*n.* 東方

The sun rises in the *east*.

easy〔'izɪ〕*adj.* 容易的

Finishing the work in an hour is not *easy*.

eat ﹝ it ﹞ *v.* 吃
Do you have something to *eat*?

egg ﹝ ɛg ﹞ *n.* 蛋
I had fried rice and *eggs* for breakfast.

eight ﹝ et ﹞ *n.* 八
Four plus four is *eight*.

eighteen ﹝ e'tin ﹞ *n.* 十八
Mark has worked in banks since he was
eighteen.

eighth ﹝ etθ ﹞ *adj.* 第八的
Today is the *eighth* of August.

eighty ﹝ 'etɪ ﹞ *adj.* 八十個
There are *eighty* people in the room.

either ﹝ 'iðɚ ﹞ *adj.* 兩者之一的
I don't have *either* a cat or a dog.

elementary school *n.* 小學
  (= *primary school*)
He didn't finish *elementary school*.

elephant ﹝ 'ɛləfənt ﹞ *n.* 大象
Elephants are found in Asia and Africa.

eleven 〔 ɪ'lɛvən 〕 *n.* 十一
Eleven comes after the number ten.

else 〔 ɛls 〕 *adv.* 別的；另外
What *else* can I do?

e-mail 〔'i͵mel 〕 *adj.* 電子郵件
You can contact me by *e-mail*.

end 〔 ɛnd 〕 *n.* 末尾；結束
Sara arrived home at the *end* of last week.

engineer 〔͵ɛndʒə'nɪr 〕 *n.* 工程師
The car was designed by *engineers*.

English 〔'ɪŋglɪʃ 〕 *n.* 英語
Ellen learns *English* every Sunday.

enjoy 〔 ɪn'dʒɔɪ 〕 *v.* 享受；喜歡
How did you *enjoy* your trip?

enough 〔 ə'nʌf 〕 *adj.* 足夠的
Have you got *enough* money to pay for this meal?

enter 〔'ɛntɚ 〕 *v.* 進入
Don't *enter* the room!

envelope (ˈɛnvəˌlop) *n.* 信封
Nancy forgot to write the address on the envelope.

eraser (ɪˈresɚ) *n.* 橡皮擦
My mother bought me a new *eraser*.

eve (iv) *n.* 前夕
Christmas *Eve* is a happy time for children.

even (ˈivən) *adv.* 甚至
I have no money. I can't *even* ride the bus.

evening (ˈivnɪŋ) *n.* 傍晚
The sun sets in the *evening*.

ever (ˈɛvɚ) *adv.* 曾經
Have you *ever* seen a lion?

every (ˈɛvrɪ) *adj.* 每一
I get up at six *every* morning.

everybody (ˈɛvrɪˌbɑdɪ) *pron.* 每個人
Everybody knows him as a singer.

everyone (ˈɛvrɪˌwʌn) *pron.* 每個人
Everyone wants to attend the concert.

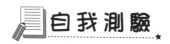

自我測驗

- ☐ dollar   _____
- ☐ dozen   _____
- ☐ draw   _____
- ☐ dress   _____
- ☐ drink   _____

- ☐ dry   _____
- ☐ early   _____
- ☐ earth   _____
- ☐ eat   _____
- ☐ elephant   _____

- ☐ e-mail   _____
- ☐ enjoy   _____
- ☐ eraser   _____
- ☐ even   _____
- ☐ ever   _____

Check List

1. 洋娃娃　　d _____*doll*_____ l
2. 向　下　　d _____ n
3. 抽　屜　　d _____ r
4. 開　車　　d _____ e
5. 掉　落　　d _____ p

6. 每一個　　e _____ h
7. 東　方　　e _____ t
8. 第八的　　e _____ h
9. 別　的　　e _____ e
10. 末　尾　　e _____ d

11. 工程師　　e _____ r
12. 足夠的　　e _____ h
13. 進　入　　e _____ r
14. 信　封　　e _____ e
15. 傍　晚　　e _____ g

everything ('εvrɪ,θɪŋ) *pron.* 一切事物
How is *everything*?

example (ɪg'zæmpl̩) *n.* 例子
Here is another *example*.

excellent ('εkslənt) *adj.* 優秀的
She is an *excellent* teacher.

except (ɪk'sεpt) *prep.* 除了…之外
I like all animals *except* snakes.

excited (ɪk'saɪtɪd) *adj.* 興奮的
Why are you so *excited* today?

exciting (ɪk'saɪtɪŋ) *adj.* 令人興奮的
What an *exciting* race it was!

excuse (ɪk'skjuz) *v.* 原諒
Excuse me for what I said to you yesterday.

exercise ('εksə,saɪz) *n.* 運動
My father gets a lot of *exercise* every evening.

expensive (ɪk'spεnsɪv) *adj.* 昂貴的
A new car is very *expensive*.

experience (ɪk'spɪrɪəns) *n.* 經驗
He has no *experience* in teaching English.

eye 〔 aɪ 〕 *n.* 眼睛

She has beautiful blue *eyes*.

F f

face 〔 fes 〕 *n.* 臉

Look into the mirror and you can see your own *face*.

fact 〔 fækt 〕 *n.* 事實

A *fact* is something that is true.

factory 〔'fæktrɪ 〕 *n.* 工廠

The children are going to visit a car *factory*.

fail 〔 fel 〕 *v.* 失敗

Our plan has *failed*.

fall 〔 fɔl 〕 *v.* 落下

The rain is *falling* down from the sky.

family 〔'fæməlɪ 〕 *n.* 家庭；家人

How is your *family*?

famous 〔'feməs 〕 *adj.* 有名的

Many people visit the *famous* mountain.

fan 〔 fæn 〕 *n.* 球迷；歌迷；影迷
He is a baseball *fan*.

far 〔 fɑr 〕 *adj.* 遠的
The post office is not *far* from here.

farm 〔 fɑrm 〕 *n.* 農場
People keep animals on a *farm*.

farmer 〔 'fɑrmɚ 〕 *n.* 農夫
Mr. Smith is a *farmer*.

fast 〔 fæst 〕 *adv.* 快
Don't drive too *fast*.

fat 〔 fæt 〕 *adj.* 胖的
Her cat is very *fat* because it eats too much.

father 〔 'fɑðɚ 〕 *n.* 父親 (= *dad*)
Jonathan is a good *father*.

favorite 〔 'fevərɪt 〕 *adj.* 最喜愛的
White chocolate is my *favorite* snack.

February 〔 'fɛbru,ɛrɪ 〕 *n.* 二月
February is the second month of the year.

feed 〔 fid 〕 *v.* 餵
We *feed* the birds every day.

feel ﹝fil﹞ *v.* 覺得
I *feel* happy because I am playing with friends.

festival ﹝'fɛstəvḷ﹞ *n.* 節日
Christmas is an important church *festival*.

fever ﹝'fivɚ﹞ *n.* 發燒
He has a little *fever*.

few ﹝fju﹞ *adj.* 很少的
There were *few* people in the streets.

fifteen ﹝fɪf'tin﹞ *n.* 十五
They got their I.D. cards at the age of *fifteen*.

fifth ﹝fɪfθ﹞ *adj.* 第五的
He is the *fifth* person to ask me the question.

fifty ﹝'fɪftɪ﹞ *adj.* 五十個
There are *fifty* students in our class.

fight ﹝faɪt﹞ *v.* 打架
Dogs always *fight* with cats.

fill ﹝fɪl﹞ *v.* 裝滿
He *filled* my glass with water.

finally ﹝'faɪnḷɪ﹞ *adv.* 最後
It was difficult, but I *finally* finished the work.

find ﹝ faɪnd ﹞ *v.* 找到
The doctor can't *find* the cause of his illness.

fine ﹝ faɪn ﹞ *adj.* 美好的
The weather is *fine*, isn't it?

finger ﹝'fɪŋɚ﹞ *n.* 手指
We have five *fingers* on each hand.

finish ﹝'fɪnɪʃ﹞ *v.* 完成
I'll *finish* this work at nine o'clock.

fire ﹝ faɪr ﹞ *n.* 火
Are you afraid of *fire*?

first ﹝ fɝst ﹞ *adj.* 第一的
The *first* person to arrive is John.

fish ﹝ fɪʃ ﹞ *n.* 魚
They caught several *fish*.

fisherman ﹝'fɪʃəmən﹞ *n.* 漁夫
A *fisherman* catches fish every day.

five ﹝ faɪv ﹞ *adj.* 五
Children go to school *five* days a week.

fix ﹝ fɪks ﹞ *v.* 修理
The machine needs to be *fixed*.

floor ﹝ flor ﹞ *n.* 地板；樓層

This elevator stops at every *floor*.

flower ﹝'flauə﹞ *n.* 花

People give *flowers* on Valentine's Day.

flute ﹝ flut ﹞ *n.* 笛子

Jason asked his mother to buy a *flute* for him.

fly ﹝ flaɪ ﹞ *v.* 飛

A bird *flies* in the sky.

follow ﹝'falo﹞ *v.* 遵守

Students must *follow* rules.

food ﹝ fud ﹞ *n.* 食物

Without *food*, people cannot live.

foot ﹝ fʊt ﹞ *n.* 腳；英呎

Wendy hurt her left *foot*.

for ﹝ fɔr ﹞ *prep.* 給…

This apple is *for* Anne.

foreign ﹝'fɔrɪn﹞ *adj.* 外國的

Our new classmate has a *foreign* accent.

foreigner ﹝'fɔrɪnə﹞ *n.* 外國人

For a *foreigner*, your Chinese is pretty good.

自我測驗

- ☐ excellent _____
- ☐ except _____
- ☐ exciting _____
- ☐ experience _____
- ☐ fact _____

- ☐ fail _____
- ☐ famous _____
- ☐ favorite _____
- ☐ festival _____
- ☐ fight _____

- ☐ find _____
- ☐ fix _____
- ☐ floor _____
- ☐ flute _____
- ☐ foreigner _____

Check List

1. 例　子　　e ___example___ e
2. 興奮的　　e _____ d
3. 昂貴的　　e _____ e
4. 工　廠　　f _____ y
5. 落　下　　f _____ l
6. 農　場　　f _____ m
7. 餵　　　　f _____ d
8. 裝　滿　　f _____ l
9. 最　後　　f _____ y
10. 美好的　　f _____ e
11. 完　成　　f _____ h
12. 漁　夫　　f _____ n
13. 遵　守　　f _____ w
14. 食　物　　f _____ d
15. 外國的　　f _____ n

forget (fəˋgɛt) *v.* 忘記
Robert *forgot* to bring his book to school.

fork (fɔrk) *n.* 叉子
When we eat, we use *forks* and knives.

forty (ˋfɔrtɪ) *n.* 四十
Forty comes after the number thirty-nine.

four (for) *adj.* 四個
There are *four* people in my family.

fourteen (ˋforˋtin) *adj.* 十四的
Jessie is *fourteen* this year.

fourth (forθ) *adj.* 第四個
You are the *fourth* person to arrive.

fox (fɑks) *n.* 狐狸
Peter found a *fox* in the forest yesterday.

free (fri) *adj.* 免費的；自由的
There is no *free* lunch in this world.

French fries   *n.* 薯條
Mary is eating *French fries*.

fresh (frɛʃ) *adj.* 新鮮的
The cake is very *fresh*.

Friday ('fraɪde) *n.* 星期五
Friday night is the best time to go out.

friend (frɛnd) *n.* 朋友
Everyone needs a *friend* to share his feelings with.

friendly ('frɛndlɪ) *adj.* 友善的
My teacher is very *friendly* to us.

frisbee ('frɪzbi) *n.* 飛盤
He threw me the *frisbee*.

frog (frɑg) *n.* 青蛙
Frogs are jumping in the rain.

from (frɑm) *prep.* 從…
Andy came *from* Japan.

front (frʌnt) *n.* 前面
Don't park your car in *front* of the building.

fruit (frut) *n.* 水果
Strawberries are my favorite *fruit*.

fry (fraɪ) *v.* 油炸
She *fried* a fish.

full 〔 fʊl 〕 *adj.* 充滿的
This river is *full* of fish.

fun 〔 fʌn 〕 *n.* 樂趣
I had so much *fun* at the party last night.

funny 〔'fʌnɪ 〕 *adj.* 好玩的
There's something *funny* about it.

future 〔'fjutʃɚ 〕 *n.* 未來
Ronald will become a doctor in the *future*.

G g

game 〔 gem 〕 *n.* 遊戲
Children like to play *games*.

garbage 〔'gɑrbɪdʒ 〕 *n.* 垃圾
We must take out the *garbage* at 9:00.

garden 〔'gɑrdn̩ 〕 *n.* 花園
Grandpa usually spends his free time in the
garden.

gas 〔 gæs 〕 *n.* 瓦斯
Mother cooks with *gas*.

gate 〔 get 〕 *n.* 大門
The castle's *gate* is very high.

get〔gɛt〕v. 得到
I hope to *get* some letters from him.

ghost〔gost〕n. 鬼
Do you believe in *ghosts*?

giant〔'dʒaɪənt〕n. 巨人
The basketball players on this team are all
giants.

gift〔gɪft〕n. 禮物
I got a *gift* from my teacher.

girl〔gɜl〕n. 女孩
Tina is a very clever *girl*.

give〔gɪv〕v. 給
Maria *gives* me a present every Christmas.

glad〔glæd〕adj. 高興的
I'm *glad* to see you again.

glass〔glæs〕n. 玻璃杯
Can you give me a *glass* of water, please?

glasses〔'glæsɪz〕n. pl. 眼鏡
I need *glasses* when I read.

glove 〔 glʌv 〕 *n.* 手套
Baseball players need to wear *gloves*.

go 〔 go 〕 *v.* 去
Justin *goes* to school every day.

goat 〔 got 〕 *n.* 山羊
Goats make funny sounds.

good 〔 gʊd 〕 *adj.* 好的
Uncle Andrew is a *good* man.

good-bye 〔 gʊd'baɪ 〕 *interj.* 再見
(= *goodbye; bye*)
Good-bye. See you tomorrow.

goose 〔 gus 〕 *n.* 鵝
The farmer is running after the *goose*.

grade 〔 gred 〕 *n.* 成績
Mary always got high *grades* in school.

gram 〔 græm 〕 *n.* 公克
Mom asked me to buy 200 *grams* of sugar.

grandfather 〔'grænd͵fɑðɚ 〕 *n.* 祖父
(= *grandpa*)
My *grandfather* died when I was young.

grandmother (ˈgrændˌmʌðɚ) *n.* 祖母
(= *grandma*)
My *grandmother* is still alive.

grape (grep) *n.* 葡萄
Wine is made from *grapes*.

grass (græs) *n.* 草
It's good to cut *grass* once a week.

gray (gre) *n.* 灰色
Gray is the color of an elephant.

great (gret) *adj.* 大的
New York is a *great* city.

green (grin) *n.* 綠色
Green is the color of grass.

ground (graʊnd) *n.* 地面
She lay on the *ground*.

group (grup) *n.* 團體
In class, we form *groups* to do different things.

grow (gro) *v.* 種植
The farmer *grows* vegetables on his farm.

- ☐ forget _____
- ☐ fox _____
- ☐ free _____
- ☐ front _____
- ☐ full _____

- ☐ garbage _____
- ☐ gate _____
- ☐ giant _____
- ☐ give _____
- ☐ glasses _____

- ☐ glove _____
- ☐ goose _____
- ☐ grape _____
- ☐ great _____
- ☐ group _____

Check List

1. 叉　子　　f _____ *fork* _____ k
2. 新鮮的　　f _____ h
3. 友善的　　f _____ y
4. 水　果　　f _____ t
5. 樂　趣　　f _____ n

6. 未　來　　f _____ e
7. 花　園　　g _____ n
8. 得　到　　g _____ t
9. 禮　物　　g _____ t
10. 高興的　　g _____ d

11. 山　羊　　g _____ t
12. 成　績　　g _____ e
13. 灰　色　　g _____ y
14. 地　面　　g _____ d
15. 種　植　　g _____ w

guava (ˈgwɑvə) *n.* 芭樂
Kate likes to eat *guavas*.

guess (gɛs) *v.* 猜測
Can you *guess* my age?

guitar (gɪˈtɑr) *n.* 吉他
John plays the *guitar* very well.

guy (gaɪ) *n.* 人；傢伙
Mr. Johnson is a nice *guy*.

gym (dʒɪm) *n.* 體育館；健身房
We play basketball in a *gym*.

H h

habit (ˈhæbɪt) *n.* 習慣
The boy has very good *habits*.

hair (hɛr) *n.* 頭髮
Rose has long black *hair*.

half (hæf) *n.* 一半
Half of the boys in this room are my friends.

Halloween (ˌhæloˈin) *n.* 萬聖節前夕
Halloween is on October 31.

ham 〔 hæm 〕 *n.* 火腿
I had *ham* and eggs for my breakfast.

hamburger 〔'hæmbɜgə 〕 *n.* 漢堡
I think I'll have a *hamburger*.

hand 〔 hænd 〕 *n.* 手
We use our *hands* to do a lot of things.

handsome 〔'hænsəm 〕 *adj.* 英俊的
Todd is a *handsome* man.

hang 〔 hæŋ 〕 *v.* 懸掛
She *hung* the picture on the wall.

happen 〔'hæpən 〕 *v.* 發生
What will *happen* next?

happy 〔'hæpɪ 〕 *adj.* 高興的
Charlie is *happy* to see his mother again.

hard 〔 hɑrd 〕 *adj.* 困難的
It is a *hard* question to answer.

hard-working 〔'hɑrd'wɜkɪŋ 〕 *adj.* 勤勉的；
用功的
Bob is a *hard-working* person.

has 〔 hæz 〕 v. 有【have 的第三人稱單數】
Joe *has* his own house near the river.

hat 〔 hæt 〕 n. 帽子
My mother bought me a red *hat*.

hate 〔 het 〕 v. 討厭
My brother *hates* snakes.

have 〔 hæv 〕 v. 有
I *have* two pens and three pencils.

he 〔 hi 〕 pron. 他
He is a teacher in a senior high school.

head 〔 hɛd 〕 n. 頭
Lucy wears a hat on her *head*.

headache 〔 'hɛd,ek 〕 n. 頭痛
Sandy has a bad *headache*.

health 〔 hɛlθ 〕 n. 健康
Nothing is better than having good *health*.

healthy 〔 'hɛlθɪ 〕 adj. 健康的
Kate's baby is very *healthy*.

hear 〔 hɪr 〕 v. 聽見
I *heard* the birds singing.

heart ﹝hɑrt﹞ *n.* 心
My *heart* always beats very fast after running.

heat ﹝hit﹞ *n.* 熱
The *heat* from the stove is very high.

heavy ﹝'hɛvɪ﹞ *adj.* 重的
This box is very *heavy*.

hello ﹝hə'lo﹞ *interj.* 哈囉
"*Hello*" is a word of greeting.

help ﹝hɛlp﹞ *v.* 幫助
I love to *help* my mother cook.

helpful ﹝'hɛlpfəl﹞ *adj.* 樂於助人的
You're very *helpful*.

hen ﹝hɛn﹞ *n.* 母雞
My grandfather raises *hens* in the country.

her ﹝hɝ﹞ *adj.* 她的
Her seat is over there.

here ﹝hɪr﹞ *adv.* 這裡
There is no one *here* today.

hers ﹝hɝz﹞ *pron.* 她的【she 的所有格代名詞】
This is not Jane's pen; *hers* is over there.

herself ﹝ hɚ'sɛlf ﹞ *pron.* 她自己【she 的反身代名詞】
She saw *herself* in the mirror.

hey ﹝ he ﹞ *interj.* 嘿；啊
Hey, how are you doing?

hi ﹝ haɪ ﹞ *interj.* 嗨
Hi there.

hide ﹝ haɪd ﹞ *v.* 隱藏
The girl *hides* herself from her mother.

high ﹝ haɪ ﹞ *adj.* 高的
He lives on a *high* floor in that building.

hike ﹝ haɪk ﹞ *v.* 健行
I go *hiking* every Sunday morning.

hill ﹝ hɪl ﹞ *n.* 山丘
We climbed a *hill* last Sunday.

him ﹝ hɪm ﹞ *pron.* 他【he 的受格】
Henry told me to wait for *him*.

himself ﹝ hɪm'sɛlf ﹞ *pron.* 他自己【he 的反身代名詞】
David fell and hurt *himself*.

hippo ﹝ 'hɪpo ﹞ *n.* 河馬
We can see a lot of *hippos* in the zoo.

his ﹝ hɪz ﹞ *adj.* 他的
Can I borrow *his* car?

history ﹝'hɪstrɪ﹞ *n.* 歷史
History is my favorite subject.

hit ﹝ hɪt ﹞ *v.* 打
He was *hit* by the teacher because he didn't
do his homework.

hobby ﹝'hɑbɪ﹞ *n.* 嗜好
My favorite *hobby* is collecting stamps.

hold ﹝ hold ﹞ *v.* 拿著
He *holds* the bag with both hands.

holiday ﹝'hɑlə,de﹞ *n.* 假日
People don't work or go to school on a *holiday*.

home ﹝ hom ﹞ *adv.* 回家　 *n.* 家
My mother usually gets *home* at 10:00.

homework ﹝'hom,wɝk﹞ *n.* 作業
Sally cannot go out because she has to do
her *homework*.

honest ﹝'ɑnɪst﹞ *adj.* 誠實的
You need to be *honest* with yourself.

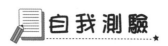

自我測驗

- ☐ guess　＿＿＿＿＿＿＿
- ☐ guy　＿＿＿＿＿＿＿
- ☐ habit　＿＿＿＿＿＿＿
- ☐ handsome　＿＿＿＿＿＿＿
- ☐ happen　＿＿＿＿＿＿＿

- ☐ hate　＿＿＿＿＿＿＿
- ☐ healthy　＿＿＿＿＿＿＿
- ☐ heat　＿＿＿＿＿＿＿
- ☐ helpful　＿＿＿＿＿＿＿
- ☐ hen　＿＿＿＿＿＿＿

- ☐ hide　＿＿＿＿＿＿＿
- ☐ hill　＿＿＿＿＿＿＿
- ☐ history　＿＿＿＿＿＿＿
- ☐ hobby　＿＿＿＿＿＿＿
- ☐ holiday　＿＿＿＿＿＿＿

Check List

1. 芭　樂　　g ____*guava*____ a

2. 吉　他　　g _____ r

3. 一　半　　h _____ f

4. 懸　掛　　h _____ g

5. 困難的　　h _____ d

6. 頭　痛　　h _____ e

7. 健　康　　h _____ h

8. 重　的　　h _____ y

9. 幫　助　　h _____ p

10. 高　的　　h _____ h

11. 河　馬　　h _____ o

12. 打　　　　h _____ t

13. 拿　著　　h _____ d

14. 作　業　　h _____ k

15. 誠實的　　h _____ t

honey ﹝'hʌnɪ﹞ *n.* 蜂蜜
Do you want some *honey* for your muffin?

hop ﹝ hɑp ﹞ *v.* 跳
The children are *hopping* on the bed.

hope ﹝ hop ﹞ *v.* 希望
I *hope* I will pass the exam.

horse ﹝ hɔrs ﹞ *n.* 馬
John rides a *horse* every morning.

hospital ﹝'hɑspɪtḷ﹞ *n.* 醫院
Doctors and nurses work in a *hospital*.

hot ﹝ hɑt ﹞ *adj.* 熱的
It's very *hot* to stand in the sun.

hot dog *n.* 熱狗
I love to eat *hot dogs* at the ballpark.

hotel ﹝ ho'tɛl ﹞ *n.* 旅館
He stayed in a *hotel* while he was in Spain.

hour ﹝ aʊr ﹞ *n.* 小時
I'll arrive at the station within an *hour*.

house ﹝ haʊs ﹞ *n.* 房子
Tom is going to buy a new *house*.

housewife (ˈhaʊsˌwaɪf) *n.* 家庭主婦
My mother is a *housewife*.

how (haʊ) *adv.* 如何
Her mother teaches her *how* to make a dress.

however (haʊˈɛvɚ) *adv.* 然而
This, *however*, is not your fault.

hundred (ˈhʌndrəd) *n.* 百
The number after ninety-nine is one *hundred*.

hungry (ˈhʌŋgrɪ) *adj.* 飢餓的
I'm *hungry* and I need to eat.

hunt (hʌnt) *v.* 打獵;獵捕
The hunters are *hunting* rabbits.

hurry (ˈhɝɪ) *v.* 匆忙
He *hurried* home to tell his mother the news.

hurt (hɝt) *v.* 傷害
My back was *hurt* in the accident.

husband (ˈhʌzbənd) *n.* 丈夫
Her *husband* has been working in France.

I i

I 〔 aɪ 〕 *pron.* 我
Am *I* right?

ice 〔 aɪs 〕 *n.* 冰
Nancy puts some *ice* in the drink.

ice cream *n.* 冰淇淋
Julia likes chocolate *ice cream*.

idea 〔 aɪ'diə 〕 *n.* 想法;點子
We should have a good *idea*.

if 〔 ɪf 〕 *conj.* 如果
If it rains, we won't go out.

important 〔 ɪm'pɔrtn̩t 〕 *adj.* 重要的
It is *important* to study English.

in 〔 ɪn 〕 *prep.* 在…裡面
He lives *in* an apartment.

inch 〔 ɪntʃ 〕 *n.* 英吋
She is three *inches* taller than me.

insect 〔'ɪnsɛkt 〕 *n.* 昆蟲
A mosquito is an *insect*.

inside ('ɪn'saɪd) *prep.* 在⋯裡面
No one is *inside* the school.

interest ('ɪntrɪst) *v.* 使感興趣
The story didn't *interest* me.

interested ('ɪntrɪstɪd) *adj.* 感興趣的
Peter is *interested* in airplanes.

interesting ('ɪntrɪstɪŋ) *adj.* 有趣的
The film is *interesting*.

Internet ('ɪntɚ,nɛt) *n.* 網際網路
If you have a computer, you can use the
Internet to find information.

interview ('ɪntɚ,vju) *n.* 面試
Jim is going to ABC company for a job
interview.

into ('ɪntu) *prep.* 到⋯之內
I threw the photo *into* the fire.

invite (ɪn'vaɪt) *v.* 邀請
I *invited* her to dinner.

is (ɪz) *v.* 是【be 的第三人稱單數】
Paul *is* 14 years old.

island ('aɪlənd) *n.* 島
An *island* is a piece of land with water all around it.

it (ɪt) *pron.* 它;牠
I bought this knife yesterday and *it* cuts very well.

its (ɪts) *pron.* 它的;牠的【it 的所有格】
This chair has lost one of *its* legs.

itself (ɪt'sɛlf) *pron.* 它自己;牠自己【it 的反身代名詞】
The monkey saw *itself* in the water.

J j

jacket ('dʒækɪt) *n.* 夾克
The waiter in the white *jacket* is very polite.

January ('dʒænjʊˌɛrɪ) *n.* 一月
January is the first month of the year.

jeans (dʒinz) *n. pl.* 牛仔褲
Most teenagers like to wear *jeans*.

job (dʒɑb) *n.* 工作
Kelly's *job* is to teach students math.

jog 〔 dʒɑg 〕 *v.* 慢跑

I like to *jog* in the morning.

join 〔 dʒɔɪn 〕 *v.* 加入

Scott *joined* the army last year.

joy 〔 dʒɔɪ 〕 *n.* 喜悅

She was filled with *joy*.

juice 〔 dʒus 〕 *n.* 果汁

Sally drinks a glass of orange *juice* every
morning.

July 〔 dʒu'laɪ 〕 *n.* 七月

Helen is going to visit her aunt in *July*.

jump 〔 dʒʌmp 〕 *v.* 跳

That big dog *jumped* over the fence.

June 〔 dʒun 〕 *n.* 六月

June is the sixth month of the year.

junior high school   *n.* 國中

I am studying in *junior high school*.

just 〔 dʒʌst 〕 *adv.* 只是；剛剛

My sister is *just* four years old, so she doesn't
go to school.

自我測驗

- [ ] honey _____
- [ ] hope _____
- [ ] hotel _____
- [ ] housewife _____
- [ ] hunt _____

- [ ] hurt _____
- [ ] idea _____
- [ ] insect _____
- [ ] interested _____
- [ ] invite _____

- [ ] island _____
- [ ] jacket _____
- [ ] job _____
- [ ] juice _____
- [ ] jump _____

Check List

1. 跳	h	*hop*	p
2. 醫　院	h		l
3. 熱　的	h		t
4. 然　而	h		r
5. 飢餓的	h		y
6. 匆　忙	h		y
7. 重要的	i		t
8. 英　吋	i		h
9. 使感興趣	i		t
10. 網際網路	I		t
11. 面　試	i		w
12. 一　月	J		y
13. 慢　跑	j		g
14. 加　入	j		n
15. 喜　悅	j		y

K k

kangaroo 〔͵kæŋgə'ru 〕 *n.* 袋鼠
The *kangaroo* is a symbol of Australia.

keep 〔 kip 〕 *v.* 保存
This book will be *kept* in the library.

key 〔 ki 〕 *n.* 鑰匙
Do not lose the house *key*.

kick 〔 kɪk 〕 *v.* 踢
The children *kicked* the ball for fun.

kid 〔 kɪd 〕 *n.* 小孩
They've got three *kids*.

kill 〔 kɪl 〕 *v.* 殺死
Lions *kill* small animals for food.

kilogram 〔'kɪlə͵græm 〕 *n.* 公斤
We measure weight in *kilograms*.

kind 〔 kaɪnd 〕 *n.* 種類
There are many *kinds* of fruit.

king 〔 kɪŋ 〕 *n.* 國王
They made him *King* of England.

kiss ﹝ kɪs ﹞ v. 親吻
She *kissed* the baby on the face.

kitchen ﹝'kɪtʃɪn﹞ n. 廚房
Mary learned to cook in the *kitchen*.

kite ﹝ kaɪt ﹞ n. 風箏
Peter has never learned to fly a *kite*.

knee ﹝ ni ﹞ n. 膝蓋
Tony fell and hurt his *knees*.

knife ﹝ naɪf ﹞ n. 刀子
Michelle used a *knife* to cut the apple.

knock ﹝ nɑk ﹞ v. 敲
The kid *knocked* on the door.

know ﹝ no ﹞ v. 知道
My mother *knows* a lot about animals.

knowledge ﹝'nɑlɪdʒ﹞ n. 知識
His *knowledge* of French is very poor.

koala ﹝ kə'ɑlə ﹞ n. 無尾熊
The *koala* comes from Australia.

L l

lake ﹝ lek ﹞ *n.* 湖
Jim lives near a *lake*.

lamp ﹝ læmp ﹞ *n.* 燈
Turn on the *lamp*, please.

land ﹝ lænd ﹞ *n.* 陸地
He traveled over *land* and sea.

language ﹝'læŋgwɪdʒ﹞ *n.* 語言
He can speak five *languages*.

lantern ﹝'læntən﹞ *n.* 燈籠
Do you know how to make a *lantern*?

large ﹝ lɑrdʒ ﹞ *adj.* 大的
We are a big family so we need a *large* house.

last ﹝ læst ﹞ *adj.* 最後的
Charles came in *last* in the race.

late ﹝ let ﹞ *adv.* 遲到；晚
Jimmy comes to school *late* every day.

later ﹝'letə﹞ *adv.* 之後
My sister will arrive here 30 minutes *later*.

laugh ﹝ læf ﹞ v. 笑
Everybody *laughs* at him because he looks funny.

lawyer (ˈlɔjɚ) n. 律師
Judy wants to be a *lawyer* in the future.

lazy (ˈlezɪ) adj. 懶惰的
My brother is very *lazy*.

lead ﹝ lid ﹞ v. 帶領
The teacher *leads* students to the playground.

leader (ˈlidɚ) n. 領導者
We chose Diane to be our class *leader*.

learn ﹝ lɝn ﹞ v. 學習
I'm going to *learn* French.

least ﹝ list ﹞ adj. 最少的
He has the *least* experience of them all.

leave ﹝ liv ﹞ v. 離開
The bus will *leave* the station in ten minutes.

left ﹝ lɛft ﹞ adj. 左邊的
He writes with his *left* hand.

leg 〔 lɛg 〕 *n.* 腿

A dog has four *legs*.

lemon 〔'lɛmən 〕 *n.* 檸檬

A *lemon* is a fruit with a very sour taste.

lend 〔 lɛnd 〕 *v.* 借（出）

Can you *lend* me your car?

less 〔 lɛs 〕 *adv.* 較少；不如【little 的比較級】

A radio costs *less* than a television.

lesson 〔'lɛsn̩ 〕 *n.* 課

Anna took a piano *lesson*.

let 〔 lɛt 〕 *v.* 讓

My father won't *let* me go to the concert.

letter 〔'lɛtɚ 〕 *n.* 信；字母

Mary has written a *letter* to her friend.

lettuce 〔'lɛtɪs 〕 *n.* 萵苣

Lettuce is a plant with large green leaves.

library 〔'laɪˌbrɛrɪ 〕 *n.* 圖書館

Don't make a loud noise in the *library*.

lid 〔 lɪd 〕 *n.* 蓋子

Take the *lid* off the pot.

lie〔 laɪ 〕*v.* 說謊
My aunt *lies* about her age.

life〔 laɪf 〕*n.* 生命；生活
Life is full of surprises.

light〔 laɪt 〕*n.* 光
When it's dark, we cannot see without *light*.

like〔 laɪk 〕*v.* 喜歡
I don't *like* pop music.

line〔 laɪn 〕*n.* 線
Draw a *line* down the center of that page.

lion〔 'laɪən 〕*n.* 獅子
Lions are wild animals that look like big cats.

lip〔 lɪp 〕*n.* 嘴唇
We move our *lips* when we speak.

list〔 lɪst 〕*n.* 名單
There were ten names on the *list*.

listen〔 'lɪsn̩ 〕*v.* 聽
Carol likes to *listen* to the music.

little〔 'lɪtl̩ 〕*adj.* 小的；少的
Your *little* sister is so cute.

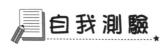自我測驗

- [ ] kangaroo _____
- [ ] keep _____
- [ ] kill _____
- [ ] kind _____
- [ ] kitchen _____

- [ ] knock _____
- [ ] know _____
- [ ] land _____
- [ ] lantern _____
- [ ] later _____

- [ ] lawyer _____
- [ ] leave _____
- [ ] lend _____
- [ ] library _____
- [ ] listen _____

Check List

1.	踢	k _____*kick*_____ k	
2.	國 王	k _____ g	
3.	膝 蓋	k _____ e	
4.	知 識	k _____ e	
5.	無尾熊	k _____ a	
6.	語 言	l _____ e	
7.	最後的	l _____ t	
8.	帶 領	l _____ d	
9.	學 習	l _____ n	
10.	腿	l _____ g	
11.	讓	l _____ t	
12.	萵 苣	l _____ e	
13.	說 謊	l _____ e	
14.	線	l _____ e	
15.	名 單	l _____ t	

live 〔 lɪv 〕 *v.* 住

He still *lives* with his parents.

living room *n.* 客廳

My father is watching TV in the *living room*.

lonely 〔'lonlɪ〕 *adj.* 寂寞的

Jimmy is a *lonely* boy.

long 〔 lɔŋ 〕 *adj.* 長的

My hair is *long*.

look 〔 lʊk 〕 *v.* 看

I'm *looking* at a small dog.

lose 〔 luz 〕 *v.* 遺失

Nancy *loses* her pens very often.

loud 〔 laʊd 〕 *adj.* 大聲的

The man speaks in a *loud* voice.

love 〔 lʌv 〕 *v.* 愛

If you *love* someone, you'll feel happy.

lovely 〔'lʌvlɪ〕 *adj.* 可愛的

Jane's puppy is *lovely*.

low 〔 lo 〕 *adj.* 低的

This chair is too *low* for Rose.

lucky ('lʌkɪ) *adj.* 幸運的
You are a *lucky* girl to have so many good friends.

lunch (lʌntʃ) *n.* 午餐
We had *lunch* at one o'clock.

M m

machine (mə'ʃin) *n.* 機器
Machines help us do things more easily.

mad (mæd) *adj.* 發瘋的
He behaves as if he were *mad*.

magic ('mædʒɪk) *adj.* 魔術的
Julie likes to watch *magic* shows.

mail (mel) *n.* 郵件
My friend contacted me by *mail*.

mailman ('mel,mæn) *n.* 郵差 (= *mail carrier*)
The *mailman* came late today.

make (mek) *v.* 製造
Don't *make* loud noises.

man (mæn) *n.* 男人
He is a very good-looking *man*.

many (ˈmɛnɪ) *adj.* 很多的
There are *many* rooms in the hotel.

map (mæp) *n.* 地圖
Have you got the *map* of Paris?

March (martʃ) *n.* 三月
March is the third month of the year.

mark (mark) *n.* 分數;記號
The teacher gave me good *marks* for my report.

marker (ˈmarkɚ) *n.* 奇異筆
The boy is drawing with a *marker*.

market (ˈmarkɪt) *n.* 市場
She sold vegetables in the *market*.

married (ˈmærɪd) *adj.* 結婚的
She is *married* to Tony.

mask (mæsk) *n.* 面具
Tom has to wear a *mask* in the school play.

mat (mæt) *n.* 墊子
Don't put your shoes on that *mat*.

math (mæθ) *n.* 數學
They were doing *math* exercises when I left.

matter〔'mætɚ〕*n.* 事情
What's the *matter* with you?

May〔me〕*n.* 五月
May is the fifth month of the year.

may〔me〕*aux.* 可以
You *may* go if you want.

maybe〔'mebɪ〕*adv.* 或許
Maybe my mother will come here next month.

me〔mi〕*pron.* 我【I 的受格】
He doesn't know *me*.

meal〔mil〕*n.* 一餐
Breakfast is our morning *meal*.

mean〔min〕*v.* 意思是
What do you *mean*?

meat〔mit〕*n.* 肉
Pork is a popular kind of *meat*.

medicine〔'mɛdəsn̩〕*n.* 藥
The doctor treated me by using *medicine*.

medium〔'midɪəm〕*adj.* 中等的
The man is of *medium* height.

meet (mit) *v.* 和～見面
I will *meet* you at the library.

meeting ('mitɪŋ) *n.* 會議
Ralph will have an important *meeting*
tomorrow.

menu ('mɛnju) *n.* 菜單
Let us see what's on the *menu* today.

middle ('mɪdḷ) *adj.* 中間的
Most Westerners' names consist of three parts,
the first name, the *middle* name, and the last
name.

might (maɪt) *aux.* 可能【may 的過去式】
He *might* not be back until tonight.

mile (maɪl) *n.* 英哩
Wendy walks two *miles* to school every day.

milk (mɪlk) *n.* 牛奶
Mary drinks a glass of *milk* every morning.

million ('mɪljən) *n.* 百萬
He made a *million* dollars.

mind (maɪnd) *n.* 心；精神
You are always on my *mind*.

mine 〔 maɪn 〕 *pron.* 我的【I 的所有格代名詞】
That wasn't his fault; it was *mine*.

minute 〔'mɪnɪt 〕 *n.* 分鐘
An hour has sixty *minutes*.

Miss 〔 mɪs 〕 *n.* 小姐
Miss Daisy is a beautiful lady.

miss 〔 mɪs 〕 *v.* 錯過;想念
John *missed* the train to Tainan.

mistake 〔 mə'stek 〕 *n.* 錯誤
Jill has made a *mistake*.

modern 〔'mɑdən 〕 *adj.* 現代的
There are a lot of *modern* buildings in New York.

moment 〔'momənt 〕 *n.* 片刻
I fell asleep for a *moment*.

Monday 〔'mʌnde 〕 *n.* 星期一
Monday is the day after Sunday.

money 〔'mʌnɪ 〕 *n.* 錢
People need *money* to live their lives.

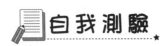

自我測驗

- [ ] live _____
- [ ] lonely _____
- [ ] lose _____
- [ ] lucky _____
- [ ] magic _____

- [ ] mailman _____
- [ ] market _____
- [ ] mask _____
- [ ] matter _____
- [ ] meal _____

- [ ] meet _____
- [ ] middle _____
- [ ] million _____
- [ ] mistake _____
- [ ] money _____

Check List

1. 長　　的　　　l ___*long*___ g
2. 大聲的　　　l _____ d
3. 低　　的　　　l _____ w
4. 機　　器　　　m _____ e
5. 製　　造　　　m _____ e

6. 地　　圖　　　m _____ p
7. 分　　數　　　m _____ k
8. 結婚的　　　m _____ d
9. 或　　許　　　m _____ e
10. 意思是　　　m _____ n

11. 中等的　　　m _____ m
12. 會　　議　　　m _____ g
13. 分　　鐘　　　m _____ e
14. 現代的　　　m _____ n
15. 片　　刻　　　m _____ t

monkey ('mʌŋkɪ) *n.* 猴子
Monkeys like to climb trees.

month (mʌnθ) *n.* 月
She has been here for a *month*.

moon (mun) *n.* 月亮
I love the light of a full *moon*.

mop (map) *v.* 用拖把拖地
I *mopped* the floor every day.

more (mor) *adj.* 更多的
James needs *more* money to buy a new house.

morning ('mɔrnɪŋ) *n.* 早上
Kim always gets up early in the *morning*.

most (most) *adj.* 大多數的
Most people like Taiwanese food.

mother ('mʌðɚ) *n.* 母親 (= *mom; mommy*)
She is a *mother* of three children.

motorcycle ('motɚ͵saɪkḷ) *n.* 摩托車
There are more and more *motorcycles* on the streets.

mountain ('mauntn̩) *n.* 山
Alex is walking to the top of the *mountain*.

mouse (maus) *n.* 老鼠
I like Mickey *Mouse* very much.

mouth (mauθ) *n.* 嘴巴
His *mouth* is full of rice.

move (muv) *v.* 移動
She *moved* away from the window.

movie ('muvɪ) *n.* 電影
I want to see a *movie* with her.

Mr. ('mɪstɚ) *n.* 先生
Mr. White teaches us music.

Mrs. ('mɪsɪz) *n.* 太太
Mrs. Brown is our math teacher.

MRT *n.* 捷運
I take the *MRT* to school every day.

Ms. (mɪz) *n.* 女士
Ms. Smith is a lovely lady.

much (mʌtʃ) *adj.* 許多的
Don't eat too *much* cake.

mud 〔 mʌd 〕*n.* 泥巴

When it rains, the ground is covered with *mud*.

museum 〔 mju'ziəm 〕*n.* 博物館

The students went to the history *museum*.

music 〔'mjuzɪk 〕*n.* 音樂

Helen listened to *music* on the radio.

must 〔 mʌst 〕*aux.* 必須

You *must* do your homework.

my 〔 maɪ 〕*adj.* 我的【I 的所有格】

Paul is *my* best friend.

myself 〔 maɪ'sɛlf 〕*pron.* 我自己【I 的反身代名詞】

I've done this job by *myself*.

N n

nail 〔 nel 〕*n.* 指甲；釘子

Henry put a *nail* in the wall to hang a picture.

name 〔 nem 〕*n.* 名字

David is the *name* of the baby.

national 〔'næʃənḷ 〕*adj.* 國家的

We should respect our *national* flag.

nature (´netʃɚ) *n.* 自然；本質
Bobby's interest was in *nature*.

near (nɪr) *prep.* 在…附近
My house is *near* the school.

neck (nɛk) *n.* 脖子
She has a long *neck*.

need (nid) *v.* 需要
I *need* to know everything before making a
decision.

neighbor (´nebɚ) *n.* 鄰居
I'm lucky to have you as my *neighbor*.

never (´nɛvɚ) *adv.* 從未
She has *never* been to a nightclub.

new (nju) *adj.* 新的
I'm going to buy a *new* car next Friday.

news (njuz) *n.* 新聞
That man was on the *news* for killing someone.

newspaper (´njuz,pepɚ) *n.* 報紙
I read *newspapers* every day.

next (nɛkst) *adj.* 下一個
Linda is the *next* person to give a speech.

nice (naɪs) *adj.* 好的
Julie is a very *nice* person.

night (naɪt) *n.* 晚上
My father hates to drive at *night*.

nine (naɪn) *adj.* 九的
Her son is *nine* years old.

nineteen ('naɪn'tin) *adj.* 十九的
Leo will be *nineteen* tomorrow.

ninety ('naɪntɪ) *n.* 九十
My grandpa died at the age of *ninety*.

ninth (naɪnθ) *adj.* 第九
My birthday is on the *ninth* of September.

no (no) *adv.* 不
No, I don't have a pencil.

nobody ('no,badɪ) *pron.* 沒有人
There is *nobody* inside the room.

nod (nad) *v.* 點頭
She *nodded* to me on the street.

noise〔 nɔɪz 〕*n.* 噪音
I hate that *noise* because it drives me crazy.

noodle〔'nudḷ 〕*n.* 麵
Chinese food is often served with rice or
noodles.

noon〔 nun 〕*n.* 正午
Lunch will be served at *noon*.

north〔 nɔrθ 〕*n.* 北方
The wind is blowing from the *north*.

nose〔 noz 〕*n.* 鼻子
The clown has his *nose* painted red.

not〔 nɑt 〕*adv.* 不
Sally is *not* here today.

note〔 not 〕*n.* 筆記　*v.* 注意
She never takes *notes* in class.

notebook〔'not,buk 〕*n.* 筆記本
I've written all the new words in my *notebook*.

nothing〔'nʌθɪŋ 〕*pron.* 什麼也沒有
I have *nothing* if I have to live without you.

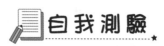

自我測驗

- ☐ monkey _____
- ☐ mop _____
- ☐ most _____
- ☐ mouth _____
- ☐ movie _____

- ☐ museum _____
- ☐ music _____
- ☐ nail _____
- ☐ nature _____
- ☐ news _____

- ☐ nice _____
- ☐ nod _____
- ☐ noodle _____
- ☐ nose _____
- ☐ note _____

Check List

1.	月　亮	m	_moon_	n
2.	早　上	m		g
3.	摩托車	m		e
4.	山	m		n
5.	移　動	m		e
6.	泥　巴	m		d
7.	必　須	m		t
8.	國家的	n		l
9.	需　要	n		d
10.	鄰　居	n		r
11.	報　紙	n		r
12.	沒有人	n		y
13.	噪　音	n		e
14.	北　方	n		h
15.	筆記本	n		k

notice (ˈnotɪs) *n.* 告示　*v.* 注意
There is a *notice* on the board.

November (noˈvɛmbə) *n.* 十一月
Paul married Mary in *November*.

now (naʊ) *adv.* 現在
We should start working *now*.

number (ˈnʌmbə) *n.* 號碼；數字
Each house has a *number*.

nurse (nɝs) *n.* 護士
A *nurse* is taking care of a patient.

O o

o'clock (əˈklɑk) *adv.* …點鐘
It's now seven *o'clock*.

October (ɑkˈtobə) *n.* 十月
October comes after September.

of (əv) *prep.* …的
I know the end *of* the story.

off (ɔf) *prep.* 離開
I can't take my eyes *off* her.

office (ˈɔfɪs) *n.* 辦公室
Lucy works in an *office*.

officer (ˈɔfəsɚ) *n.* 警官
The police *officer* stopped the car.

often (ˈɔfən) *adv.* 經常
I *often* go to the library at lunchtime.

oil (ɔɪl) *n.* 油
Pat puts *oil* in the pan to fry an egg.

OK (ˈoˈke) *adv.* 順利地;很好地
This car runs *OK*.

old (old) *adj.* 古老的
China is an *old* country.

on (ɑn) *prep.* 在⋯之上
The food is *on* the table.

once (wʌns) *adv.* 一次
Henry has been to Paris *once*.

one (wʌn) *adj.* 一個
Dolly has *one* cat and two dogs.

only (ˈonlɪ) *adj.* 唯一的
The *only* thing I can't stand is cheating.

open (ˈopən) *v.* 打開
Ben *opened* his bag to take out the books.

or (ɔr) *conj.* 或
Either one *or* two is fine.

orange (ˈɔrɪndʒ) *n.* 柳橙
Sarah bought some *oranges* at the supermarket.

order (ˈɔrdɚ) *v.* 點 (餐)
We *ordered* our dinner.

other (ˈʌðɚ) *adj.* 其他的
I have many *other* things to do.

our (aur) *adj.* 我們的【we 的所有格】
We have to carry *our* books to school every day.

ours (aurz) *pron.* 我們的【we 的所有格代名詞】
His house is larger than *ours*.

ourselves (aurˈsɛlvz) *pron.* 我們自己【we 的反身代名詞】
We bought *ourselves* a new house.

out (aut) *adv.* 到外面
Jimmy went *out* to play.

outside ('aut'saɪd) *adv.* 在外面
Many people who are *outside* wanted to get in.

over ('ovɚ) *prep.* 越過；超過
John can jump *over* that fence.

own (on) *v.* 擁有
Who *owns* this land?

ox (ɑks) *n.* 公牛 (= *bull*)
An *ox* is an animal.

P p

pack (pæk) *v.* 包裝
All clothes will be *packed* into the bag.

package ('pækɪdʒ) *n.* 包裹
Here is a *package* for you.

page (pedʒ) *n.* 頁
How many *pages* are there in this book?

paint (pent) *v.* 油漆
I *painted* my house blue.

pair (pɛr) *n.* 一雙
Lucy forgot her *pair* of shoes at school.

pants 〔 pænts 〕 *n.pl.* 褲子

I saw him in a white shirt and black *pants*.

papaya 〔 pə'paɪə 〕 *n.* 木瓜

Rose bought a *papaya* at the market.

paper 〔'pepɚ 〕 *n.* 紙

This doll is made of *paper*.

parents 〔'pɛrənts 〕 *n.pl.* 父母

Linda stays with her *parents*.

park 〔 pɑrk 〕 *v.* 停 (車)

She *parked* her car there for five minutes.

part 〔 pɑrt 〕 *n.* 部分

A leg is a *part* of the body.

party 〔'pɑrtɪ 〕 *n.* 宴會

Jimmy is going to have a birthday *party*.

pass 〔 pæs 〕 *v.* 通過

Tommy wants to *pass* this exam.

past 〔 pæst 〕 *prep.* 經過

To get to the park, you have to walk *past* the bank.

paste ﹝ pest ﹞ *n.* 漿糊
Please use *paste* to stick your picture at the top of the application form.

pay ﹝ pe ﹞ *v.* 付錢
I'll *pay* for the meal.

PE ﹝'pi'i ﹞ *n.* 體育 (= *physical education*)
We have a *PE* class today.

peach ﹝ pitʃ ﹞ *n.* 桃子
Do you want to eat *peaches*?

pear ﹝ pɛr ﹞ *n.* 西洋梨
A *pear* is a sweet and juicy fruit.

pen ﹝ pɛn ﹞ *n.* 筆
Could you lend me a *pen*, please?

pencil ﹝'pɛnsḷ ﹞ *n.* 鉛筆
Paul signs his name in *pencil*.

people ﹝'pipḷ ﹞ *n.pl.* 人
Many *people* ride the MRT at rush hour.

perhaps ﹝ pɚ'hæps ﹞ *adv.* 或許
Perhaps your book is on your desk.

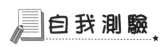

自我測驗

- ☐ notice _____
- ☐ now _____
- ☐ October _____
- ☐ office _____
- ☐ often _____

- ☐ only _____
- ☐ open _____
- ☐ order _____
- ☐ outside _____
- ☐ package _____

- ☐ papaya _____
- ☐ park _____
- ☐ pay _____
- ☐ pencil _____
- ☐ perhaps _____

Check List

1. 號　碼　n ___number___ r
2. 護　士　n _____ e
3. 警　官　o _____ r
4. 古老的　o _____ d
5. 柳　橙　o _____ e

6. 其他的　o _____ r
7. 擁　有　o _____ n
8. 包　裝　p _____ k
9. 油　漆　p _____ t
10. 紙　　　p _____ r

11. 宴　會　p _____ y
12. 通　過　p _____ s
13. 漿　糊　p _____ e
14. 桃　子　p _____ h
15. 西洋梨　p _____ r

person ('pɜsn̩) *n.* 人
There are three *persons* in the living room.

pet (pɛt) *n.* 寵物
Mike keeps a lot of *pets*.

photo ('foto) *n.* 照片 (= *photograph*)
I took a lot of *photos* on my trip.

piano (pɪ'æno) *n.* 鋼琴
Lucy played the *piano* in the concert.

pick (pɪk) *v.* 挑選
Frank *picked* a ball from the box.

picnic ('pɪknɪk) *n.* 野餐
Our family enjoyed a *picnic* on Sunday.

picture ('pɪktʃɚ) *n.* 圖畫
An artist is painting a *picture*.

pie (paɪ) *n.* 派
Elsa made a cherry *pie* by herself.

piece (pis) *n.* 一張
I gave him a *piece* of paper.

pig (pɪg) *n.* 豬
The farmer raises *pigs*.

pin ﹙ pɪn ﹚ *n.* 別針
Lisa used *pins* to hold pieces of cloth together.

pink ﹙ pɪŋk ﹚ *n.* 粉紅色
The lady wore *pink* at the party.

pipe ﹙ paɪp ﹚ *n.* 管子；煙斗；笛子
Joe is fixing the *pipe*.

pizza ﹙ˈpitsə﹚ *n.* 披薩
A *pizza* was delivered to my home.

place ﹙ ples ﹚ *n.* 地方
This is the *place* where we traveled.

plan ﹙ plæn ﹚ *v.* 計劃
Eve *planned* to study abroad.

planet ﹙ˈplænɪt﹚ *n.* 行星
Our earth is one of the *planets* in the solar system.

plant ﹙ plænt ﹚ *n.* 植物   *v.* 種植
The mango is a tropical *plant*.

plate ﹙ plet ﹚ *n.* 盤子
Can you wash those *plates*?

play 〔 ple 〕 v. 玩
They are *playing* in the park.

player 〔'pleæ 〕 n. 球員
There were five *players* on each team.

playground 〔'ple,graund 〕 n. 操場；遊樂場
A *playground* is a place for children to play.

please 〔 pliz 〕 v. 請
Would you *please* help me clean the room?

pleasure 〔'plεʒæ 〕 n. 樂趣
Playing basketball gives me great *pleasure*.

p.m. 〔'pi'εm 〕 adv. 下午
It's 5:30 *p.m.*

pocket 〔'pɑkɪt 〕 n. 口袋
There are two *pockets* on my pants.

point 〔 pɔɪnt 〕 n. 點
What do these *points* on the map stand for?

police 〔 pə'lis 〕 n. 警方
The *police* caught the robbers.

polite 〔 pə'laɪt 〕 adj. 有禮貌的
You have to be *polite* when speaking to the teacher.

pond 〔 pɑnd 〕 *n.* 池塘
There were two dogs drinking from the *pond*.

pool 〔 pul 〕 *n.* 水池；游泳池
There is a swimming *pool* in the front yard.

poor 〔 pʊr 〕 *adj.* 窮的
He is too *poor* to buy a computer.

popcorn 〔 'pɑp,kɔrn 〕 *n.* 爆米花
I love to eat *popcorn* when watching TV.

popular 〔 'pɑpjələ 〕 *adj.* 受歡迎的
"Snow White" is a very *popular* story.

pork 〔 pɔrk 〕 *n.* 豬肉
I hate eating *pork*.

possible 〔 'pɑsəbḷ 〕 *adj.* 可能的
He had tried every *possible* way to find her.

post office *n.* 郵局
You can buy stamps at the *post office*.

postcard 〔 'post,kɑrd 〕 *n.* 明信片
I sent a *postcard* to my friend.

pot 〔 pɑt 〕 *n.* 鍋子
The *pot* is broken, isn't it?

pound (paʊnd) *n.* 磅
The tomato weighs four *pounds*.

power ('paʊɚ) *n.* 力量
Holding this heavy box requires a lot of *power*.

practice ('præktɪs) *v.* 練習
Helen *practices* basketball every afternoon.

pray (pre) *v.* 祈禱
John *prays* before he goes to bed.

prepare (prɪ'pɛr) *v.* 準備
Fred *prepares* his own breakfast in the
morning.

present ('prɛznt) *n.* 禮物；現在
This guitar would be a great Christmas *present*.

pretty ('prɪtɪ) *adj.* 漂亮的
Emma is a *pretty* girl.

price (praɪs) *n.* 價格
She is looking at the *price* of the dress.

prince (prɪns) *n.* 王子
A *prince* is the son of a king and a queen.

princess (ˈprɪnsɪs) *n.* 公主
A *princess* is the daughter of a king and a queen.

prize (praɪz) *n.* 獎；獎品
He won the first *prize*.

problem (ˈprɑbləm) *n.* 問題
They have a *problem* they cannot solve.

program (ˈprogræm) *n.* 節目
"Super Sunday" is my favorite TV *program*.

proud (praʊd) *adj.* 驕傲的
They are *proud* that she is doing well at school.

public (ˈpʌblɪk) *adj.* 公共的
You mustn't do that in a *public* place.

pull (pʊl) *v.* 拉
I *pulled* her up from the river.

pumpkin (ˈpʌmpkɪn) *n.* 南瓜
People make *pumpkin* lanterns on Halloween.

puppy (ˈpʌpɪ) *n.* 小狗
A lot of *puppies* were sold at the night market.

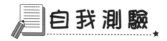

- [ ] pet _____
- [ ] pick _____
- [ ] picture _____
- [ ] place _____
- [ ] plant _____

- [ ] player _____
- [ ] point _____
- [ ] pool _____
- [ ] poor _____
- [ ] pot _____

- [ ] pray _____
- [ ] price _____
- [ ] prize _____
- [ ] proud _____
- [ ] pumpkin _____

Check List

1. 照　片　　p ____photo____ o
2. 鋼　琴　　p _____ o
3. 披　薩　　p _____ a
4. 計　劃　　p _____ n
5. 行　星　　p _____ t

6. 樂　趣　　p _____ e
7. 警　方　　p _____ e
8. 有禮貌的　p _____ e
9. 受歡迎的　p _____ r
10. 可能的　　p _____ e

11. 力　量　　p _____ r
12. 練　習　　p _____ e
13. 準　備　　p _____ e
14. 節　目　　p _____ m
15. 公共的　　p _____ c

purple 〔'pɜpl̩〕 *adj.* 紫色的
She has a *purple* shirt.

push 〔puʃ〕 *v.* 推
They *pushed* him into the car.

put 〔put〕 *v.* 放
He *puts* down a heavy bag.

Q q

quarter 〔'kwɔrtɚ〕 *n.* 四分之一
He has walked a *quarter* of a mile.

queen 〔kwin〕 *n.* 皇后
The *queen* is the king's wife.

question 〔'kwɛstʃən〕 *n.* 問題
May I ask you a *question*?

quick 〔kwɪk〕 *adj.* 快的
I'm not a *quick* runner.

quiet 〔'kwaɪət〕 *adj.* 安靜的
Sally is a *quiet* child.

quite 〔kwaɪt〕 *adv.* 非常
He is *quite* sick, so he can't go to school today.

quiz 〔kwɪz〕 *n.* 小考
We'll have a *quiz* in math class tomorrow.

R r

rabbit 〔'ræbɪt〕 *n.* 兔子
Adam feeds his *rabbits* twice a day.

race 〔res〕 *n.* 賽跑；種族
He came in second in the *race*.

radio 〔'redɪˌo〕 *n.* 收音機
My father listens to the *radio* early in the
morning.

railway 〔'relˌwe〕 *n.* 鐵路
Don't walk along the *railway*.

rain 〔ren〕 *n.* 雨   *v.* 下雨
The ground is wet because of the *rain*.

rainbow 〔'renˌbo〕 *n.* 彩虹
There are seven colors in the *rainbow*.

rainy 〔'renɪ〕 *adj.* 下雨的
Today is a *rainy* day.

raise 〔rez〕 *v.* 提高；舉起
Jennifer is the first to *raise* her hand.

rat 〔 ræt 〕 *n.* 老鼠
The *rats* have made holes in those bags of rice.

read 〔 rid 〕 *v.* 閱讀
Dad *reads* the newspaper every morning.

ready 〔'rɛdɪ 〕 *adj.* 準備好的
Karen is not *ready* for the exam.

real 〔'riəl 〕 *adj.* 眞的
This apple is not *real*.

really 〔'riəlɪ 〕 *adv.* 事實上
He looked poor but he is *really* rich.

recorder 〔 rɪ'kɔrdɚ 〕 *n.* 錄音機
Who knows how to use that *recorder*?

red 〔 rɛd 〕 *adj.* 紅色的
Blood is *red* in color.

refrigerator 〔 rɪ'frɪdʒə,retɚ 〕 *n.* 冰箱
Keep that cake in the *refrigerator*, please.

remember 〔 rɪ'mɛmbɚ 〕 *v.* 記得
I can't *remember* where I put the pen.

repeat 〔 rɪ'pit 〕 v. 重複說
The teacher *repeated* his words to the class.

reporter 〔 rɪ'portɚ 〕 n. 記者
My father was a *reporter*.

rest 〔 rɛst 〕 v. 休息
After doing exercise, Joe sat down to *rest*.

restaurant 〔'rɛstərənt 〕 n. 餐廳
A lot of people have their lunch in the
restaurant.

restroom 〔'rɛst,rum 〕 n. 洗手間 (= *rest room*)
Let's ask the person where the *restroom* is.

rice 〔 raɪs 〕 n. 米飯
The children like to eat *rice* more than noodles.

rich 〔 rɪtʃ 〕 adj. 有錢的
Bill Gates is a *rich* man.

ride 〔 raɪd 〕 v. 騎
The small boy is *riding* a bicycle.

right 〔 raɪt 〕 adj. 正確的；右邊的
Show me the *right* way to do it.

ring 〔 rɪŋ 〕 v. (鈴) 響   n. 戒指
Didn't the telephone *ring*?

rise 〔 raɪz 〕 v. 上升
The sun *rises* in the east.

river ('rɪvɚ) n. 河流
Rivers carry water into the sea or a lake.

road 〔 rod 〕 n. 道路
Don't play on the *road*.

R.O.C. n. 中華民國 (= *Republic of China*)
Taiwan is the home of the *R.O.C.*

robot ('robət) n. 機器人
A *robot* can do things like a human being.

rock 〔 rɑk 〕 n. 岩石   v. 搖動
The house was built on a *rock*.

roll 〔 rol 〕 v. 滾動
The ball *rolled* over and over.

roller skate ('rolɚ‚sket) n. 輪式溜冰鞋
(= *roller blade*)
He is wearing his *roller skates*.

room〔rum〕*n.* 房間
Walter lives in a big house with many *rooms*.

rope〔rop〕*n.* 繩子
Edward uses a *rope* to tie the boat.

rose〔roz〕*n.* 玫瑰
Roses are beautiful, sweet-smelling flowers.

round〔raʊnd〕*adj.* 圓的
Mary is wearing *round* glasses.

row〔ro〕*n.* 排　*v.* 划（船）
We have two *rows* of teeth.

rule〔rul〕*v.* 統治　*n.* 規則
The king *ruled* the country for many years.

ruler〔'rulɚ〕*n.* 尺
He drew lines with a *ruler*.

run〔rʌn〕*v.* 跑
Kate can *run* very fast.

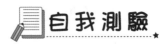
自我測驗

- [ ] push   _____
- [ ] put   _____
- [ ] question   _____
- [ ] quiet   _____
- [ ] railway   _____

- [ ] raise   _____
- [ ] read   _____
- [ ] really   _____
- [ ] remember   _____
- [ ] restaurant   _____

- [ ] right   _____
- [ ] roll   _____
- [ ] rose   _____
- [ ] row   _____
- [ ] run   _____

Check List

1. 快 的   q _____quick_____ k
2. 非 常   q _____ e
3. 賽跑；種族   r _____ e
4. 下雨的   r _____ y
5. 準備好的   r _____ y
6. 冰 箱   r _____ r
7. 重複說   r _____ t
8. 記 者   r _____ r
9. 有錢的   r _____ h
10. （鈴）響   r _____ g
11. 上 升   r _____ e
12. 機器人   r _____ t
13. 繩 子   r _____ e
14. 圓 的   r _____ d
15. 統 治   r _____ e

S s

sad 〔 sæd 〕 *adj.* 悲傷的
I always cry whenever I see a *sad* movie.

safe 〔 sef 〕 *adj.* 安全的
This street is *safe* for walking.

sail 〔 sel 〕 *v.* 航行
The ship *sails* slowly into the harbor.

salad 〔'sæləd 〕 *n.* 沙拉
Salad is a healthy food.

sale 〔 sel 〕 *n.* 出售；特價；拍賣
Mr. Dawson's car is for *sale*.

salesman 〔'selzmən 〕 *n.* 售貨員
Robert is a car *salesman*.

salt 〔 sɔlt 〕 *n.* 鹽
Pass me the *salt*, please.

same 〔 sem 〕 *adj.* 相同的
We always go to the *same* place after work.

sandwich 〔'sændwɪtʃ 〕 *n.* 三明治
We can find fish *sandwiches* at McDonald's.

Saturday ('sætə‑de) *n.* 星期六
Saturday comes after Friday.

save (sev) *v.* 拯救
Jacky *saved* Judy from drowning.

say (se) *v.* 說
No one can *say* this in French.

scared (skɛrd) *adj.* 受驚嚇的
She was *scared* by the strange noise.

school (skul) *n.* 學校
We go to *school* five days a week.

science ('saɪəns) *n.* 科學
Science is verified knowledge.

scooter ('skutɚ) *n.* 速克達機車
Jimmy rides his *scooter* to work every day.

screen (skrin) *n.* 螢幕
There is a spot on the TV *screen*.

sea (si) *n.* 海
Is the *sea* here warm enough for swimming?

season ('sizn̩) *n.* 季節
There are four *seasons* in a year.

seat 〔 sit 〕 *n.* 座位
Alisa gave her *seat* on the bus to an old woman.

second 〔'sɛkənd 〕 *adj.* 第二的　*n.* 秒
The *second* prize was given to William.

secretary 〔'sɛkrə,tɛrɪ 〕 *n.* 秘書
She is the private *secretary* of my boss.

see 〔 si 〕 *v.* 看見
I can't *see* the blackboard clearly.

seed 〔 sid 〕 *n.* 種子
We sowed vegetable *seeds* in the garden.

seesaw 〔'si,sɔ 〕 *n.* 蹺蹺板
The kids are playing on a *seesaw* at the park.

seldom 〔'sɛldəm 〕 *adv.* 很少
I *seldom* go out at night.

sell 〔 sɛl 〕 *v.* 賣
Judy *sells* her land to pay debts.

send 〔 sɛnd 〕 *v.* 寄；送
I *sent* a greeting card to my sister.

senior high school *n.* 高中
My brother studies in a famous *senior high school*.

sentence ('sɛntəns) *n.* 句子
Please make a *sentence* with the word.

September (sɛp'tɛmbɚ) *n.* 九月
Lisa's birthday is in *September*.

serious ('sɪrɪəs) *adj.* 嚴重的；認眞的
Tom had a *serious* car accident yesterday.

set (sɛt) *v.* 設定   *n.* 一套
We must *set* the time for the meeting.

seven ('sɛvən) *adj.* 七個
There are *seven* days in a week.

seventeen (ˌsɛvən'tin) *adj.* 十七的
Sam's elder brother is *seventeen* years old.

seventh ('sɛvənθ) *adj.* 第七的
This is Beethoven's *seventh* symphony.

seventy ('sɛvəntɪ) *adj.* 七十個
There are *seventy* people in my class.

several (ˈsɛvərəl) *adj.* 好幾個
Several boys took part in the race.

shake (ʃek) *v.* 搖動
You should *shake* the can before drinking.

shall (ʃæl) *aux.* 將
After 10:00 p.m., Nancy *shall* call you again.

shape (ʃep) *n.* 形狀
The shell has a strange *shape*.

share (ʃɛr) *v.* 分享
John *shared* his popcorn with me.

shark (ʃɑrk) *n.* 鯊魚
No one can catch the *shark*.

sharp (ʃɑrp) *adj.* 銳利的
The knife is very *sharp*.

she (ʃi) *pron.* 她
She is a nurse.

sheep (ʃip) *n.* 羊
John keeps a lot of *sheep*.

shine (ʃaɪn) *v.* 照耀
The sun *shines* brightly.

ship (ʃɪp) *n.* 船
Ships carry passengers over the sea.

shirt (ʃɜt) *n.* 襯衫
This shop sells sports *shirts*.

shoes (ʃuz) *n. pl.* 鞋子
I wore a new pair of *shoes* this morning.

shop (ʃɑp) *n.* 商店
This flower *shop* opens at 6:00 a.m.

shopkeeper ('ʃɑpˏkipɚ) *n.* 商店老闆
The *shopkeeper* manages this shop very well.

short (ʃɔrt) *adj.* 短的
He finished his homework in a very *short* time.

shorts (ʃɔrts) *n. pl.* 短褲
She wore *shorts* to play volleyball.

should (ʃʊd) *aux.* 應該
You *should* take a rest.

shoulder ('ʃoldɚ) *n.* 肩膀
His *shoulder* was hurt in an accident.

shout (ʃaʊt) *v.* 吼叫
My friend *shouted* at me yesterday.

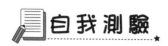自我測驗

- [ ] sail _____
- [ ] sale _____
- [ ] same _____
- [ ] science _____
- [ ] season _____

- [ ] secretary _____
- [ ] sell _____
- [ ] sentence _____
- [ ] send _____
- [ ] sentence _____

- [ ] set _____
- [ ] several _____
- [ ] shape _____
- [ ] shine _____
- [ ] shout _____

Check List

1. 安全的   s ____safe____ e
2. 售貨員   s _____ n
3. 拯　救   s _____ e
4. 受驚嚇的   s _____ d
5. 螢　幕   s _____ n

6. 種　子   s _____ d
7. 很　少   s _____ m
8. 嚴重的   s _____ s
9. 搖　動   s _____ e
10. 分　享   s _____ e

11. 鯊　魚   s _____ k
12. 銳利的   s _____ p
13. 襯　衫   s _____ t
14. 商店老闆   s _____ r
15. 肩　膀   s _____ r

show 〔 ∫o 〕 v. 給 (某人) 看 　 n. 表演
He *showed* me his album.

shy 〔 ∫aɪ 〕 *adj.* 害羞的
I'm too *shy* to speak to strangers.

sick 〔 sɪk 〕 *adj.* 生病的
He is *sick* with a cold.

side 〔 saɪd 〕 *n.* 邊
You must walk on one *side* of the road.

sidewalk 〔'saɪd,wɔk 〕 *n.* 人行道
She fell on the icy *sidewalk*.

sight 〔 saɪt 〕 *n.* 視力；景象
Kelly has good *sight*.

sign 〔 saɪn 〕 *n.* 告示牌 　 v. 簽名
The *sign* says, "No Smoking."

simple 〔'sɪmpl̩ 〕 *adj.* 簡單的
This book is written in *simple* English.

since 〔 sɪns 〕 *prep.* 自從
It has been raining *since* five in the morning.

sing 〔 sɪŋ 〕 *v.* 唱歌
We often *sing* a song in music class.

singer ('sɪŋɚ) *n.* 歌手
Madonna is my favorite *singer*.

sir (sɜ) *n.* 先生
Good luck to you, *sir*.

sister ('sɪstɚ) *n.* 姊妹
I have one *sister* and two brothers.

sit (sɪt) *v.* 坐
Please *sit* down.

six (sɪks) *n.* 六
Five plus one equals *six*.

sixteen (sɪks'tin) *adj.* 十六的
Kate's brother is *sixteen* years old.

sixth (sɪksθ) *adj.* 第六的
June is the *sixth* month of the year.

sixty ('sɪkstɪ) *adj.* 六十的
My grandmother is *sixty* years old.

size (saɪz) *n.* 尺寸；大小
What *size* do you wear?

skate (sket) *v.* 溜冰
Most young people enjoy *skating*.

skirt ﹝ skɝt ﹞ *n.* 裙子
Patrick bought his girlfriend a *skirt*.

sky ﹝ skaɪ ﹞ *n.* 天空
Birds fly across the *sky*.

sleep ﹝ slip ﹞ *v.* 睡覺
Anna *sleeps* well after a long trip.

slide ﹝ slaɪd ﹞ *v.* 滑
A car *slides* along the road.

slim ﹝ slɪm ﹞ *adj.* 苗條的
She is a *slim* girl.

slow ﹝ slo ﹞ *adj.* 慢的
My watch is two minutes *slow*.

small ﹝ smɔl ﹞ *adj.* 小的
There is a *small* house behind the mountain.

smart ﹝ smɑrt ﹞ *adj.* 聰明的
Victor is explaining his *smart* idea.

smell ﹝ smɛl ﹞ *v.* 聞
Jenny *smelled* the rose with her nose.

smile ﹝ smaɪl ﹞ *v.* 微笑
Remember to *smile* when I take your picture.

smoke 〔 smok 〕 *n.* 煙   *v.* 抽煙
The kitchen was filled with black *smoke*.

snack 〔 snæk 〕 *n.* 點心;零食
Sam wants to eat a *snack* before dinner.

snake 〔 snek 〕 *n.* 蛇
Snakes have long and thin bodies.

snow 〔 sno 〕 *n.* 雪   *v.* 下雪
The *snow* came late this year.

snowman 〔'sno͵mæn 〕 *n.* 雪人
Let's build a *snowman*.

snowy 〔'snoɪ 〕 *adj.* 多雪的
We are going to have a *snowy* winter this year.

so 〔 so 〕 *adv.* 非常地
I'm *so* tired after running.

soccer 〔'sɑkɚ 〕 *n.* 足球
The boys are playing *soccer*.

socks 〔 sɑks 〕 *n. pl.* 短襪
We put on our *socks* before wearing our shoes.

sofa 〔'sofə 〕 *n.* 沙發
Mary is sitting on the *sofa* and reading a book.

soldier ('soldʒɚ) *n.* 軍人
Peter is a *soldier*.

some (sʌm) *adj.* 一些
My sister wants to drink *some* milk.

somebody ('sʌm,badı) *pron.* 有人；某人
Somebody wants to see you.

someone ('sʌm,wʌn) *pron.* 某人
I saw *someone* walking in front of your house.

something ('sʌmθɪŋ) *pron.* 某事
I had *something* to tell you, but I forgot.

sometimes ('sʌm,taɪmz) *adv.* 有時候
Sometimes it rains in the morning.

somewhere ('sʌm,hwɛr) *adv.* 某處
Fred has left his books *somewhere* in the school.

son (sʌn) *n.* 兒子
She has two *sons* and one daughter.

song (sɔŋ) *n.* 歌曲
Karen really loves to write *songs*.

soon (sun) *adv.* 很快地
I hope we will get there *soon*.

sore ﹝ sor ﹞ *adj.* 疼痛的
I have a *sore* throat.

sorry ﹝'sɔrɪ﹞ *adj.* 抱歉的
I'm *sorry* to hurt you.

sound ﹝ saʊnd ﹞ *n.* 聲音
I heard a strange *sound*.

soup ﹝ sup ﹞ *n.* 湯
Henry asked for a bowl of *soup*.

south ﹝ saʊθ ﹞ *n.* 南方
Mexico is to the *south* of the United States.

space ﹝ spes ﹞ *n.* 空間；太空
Our new house has more *space*.

spaghetti ﹝ spə'gɛtɪ ﹞ *n.* 義大利麵
He ate *spaghetti* for lunch.

speak ﹝ spik ﹞ *v.* 說
Michelle can *speak* Spanish.

special ﹝'spɛʃəl﹞ *adj.* 特別的
He surprised his wife with a *special* gift.

spell ﹝ spɛl ﹞ *v.* 拼（字）
He *spells* his name for me.

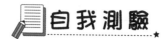

自我測驗

- [ ] show   _____
- [ ] sick   _____
- [ ] sight   _____
- [ ] sign   _____
- [ ] size   _____

- [ ] sky   _____
- [ ] slim   _____
- [ ] smell   _____
- [ ] smoke   _____
- [ ] snack   _____

- [ ] snake   _____
- [ ] soldier   _____
- [ ] song   _____
- [ ] space   _____
- [ ] spell   _____

1. 人行道　　s ____*sidewalk*____ k
2. 簡單的　　s _____ e
3. 歌　手　　s _____ r
4. 溜　冰　　s _____ e
5. 睡　覺　　s _____ p

6. 滑　　　　s _____ e
7. 聰明的　　s _____ t
8. 微　笑　　s _____ e
9. 多雪的　　s _____ y
10. 沙　發　　s _____ a

11. 一　些　　s _____ e
12. 有時候　　s _____ s
13. 疼痛的　　s _____ e
14. 聲　音　　s _____ d
15. 特別的　　s _____ l

spend 〔 spɛnd 〕 v. 花費
Nick *spends* so much money on traveling.

spider 〔'spaɪdə 〕 n. 蜘蛛
Judy is afraid of *spiders*.

spoon 〔 spun 〕 n. 湯匙
People use *spoons* for eating.

sport 〔 sport 〕 n. 運動
Soccer is the favorite *sport* of English people.

spring 〔 sprɪŋ 〕 n. 春天
Mandy will come back home in *spring*.

square 〔 skwɛr 〕 n. 正方形
The paper was cut into *square*s.

stairs 〔 stɛrz 〕 n. pl. 樓梯
Tom is going down the *stairs*.

stamp 〔 stæmp 〕 n. 郵票
He is a *stamp* collector.

stand 〔 stænd 〕 v. 站著
Don't *stand* there; I can't see the television.

star 〔 star 〕 n. 星星
There are many *stars* in the sky tonight.

start ﹝ stɑrt ﹞ *v.* 開始

The performance *started* at eight.

station ﹝'steʃən﹞ *n.* 車站

I parked my car at the *station*.

stay ﹝ ste ﹞ *v.* 暫住；停留

My sister *stays* at my apartment.

steak ﹝ stek ﹞ *n.* 牛排

The waiter is serving me *steak*.

still ﹝ stɪl ﹞ *adv.* 仍然

They *still* do not know the result.

stomach ﹝'stʌmək﹞ *n.* 胃

The food we eat goes into our *stomach*.

stop ﹝ stɑp ﹞ *v.* 停止

The car *stops* at the red light.

store ﹝ stor ﹞ *n.* 商店

Mother took us to the shoe *store* to buy shoes.

story ﹝'storɪ﹞ *n.* 故事

Harry Potter is the *story* of a little wizard.

straight ﹝ stret ﹞ *adj.* 直的

She has beautiful long *straight* hair.

strange (strendʒ) *adj.* 奇怪的
It's a *strange* story about a cat and a mouse.

stranger ('strendʒɚ) *n.* 陌生人
His dog barks at *strangers*.

straw (strɔ) *n.* 稻草；吸管
The last *straw* breaks the camel's back.

strawberry ('strɔˌbɛrɪ) *n.* 草莓
Her favorite fruit is *strawberry*.

street (strit) *n.* 街道
There is a library on the *street* where I live.

strong (strɔŋ) *adj.* 強壯的
He has *strong* arms.

student ('stjudn̩t) *n.* 學生
The teacher punished the lazy *student*.

study ('stʌdɪ) *v.* 學習；研讀
Andrew *studies* English by himself.

stupid ('stjupɪd) *adj.* 愚蠢的
Laura gave me a *stupid* idea.

subject ('sʌbdʒɪkt) *n.* 科目；主題
English is my favorite *subject*.

successful (sək'sɛsfəl) *adj.* 成功的
She has a very *successful* career.

sugar ('ʃugɚ) *n.* 糖
Kate puts *sugar* in her tea.

summer ('sʌmɚ) *n.* 夏天
Summer is one of the four seasons.

sun (sʌn) *n.* 太陽
On a clear day, the *sun* shines brightly in the sky.

Sunday ('sʌnde) *n.* 星期日
Sunday comes after Saturday.

sunny ('sʌnɪ) *adj.* 晴朗的
Yesterday was very bright and *sunny*.

supermarket ('supɚˌmarkɪt) *n.* 超級市場
Cheeses are sold in the *supermarket*.

sure (ʃʊr) *adj.* 確定的
I'm not *sure* about my answer.

surf (sɝf) *v.* 衝浪
Eric is good at *surfing*.

surprise (sə'praɪz) *v.* 使驚訝 *n.* 驚訝
We *surprised* Ann with a birthday party.

surprised 〔 səˈpraɪzd 〕 *adj.* 驚訝的
Jim was *surprised* by her gift.

sweater 〔ˈswɛtɚ 〕 *n.* 毛衣
Sweaters are usually made of wool.

sweet 〔 swit 〕 *adj.* 甜美的
Ann has a *sweet* voice.

swim 〔 swɪm 〕 *v.* 游泳
Lisa is fond of *swimming*.

swing 〔 swɪŋ 〕 *v.* 搖擺   *n.* 鞦韆
The boy is *swinging* his legs.

T t

table 〔ˈtebḷ 〕 *n.* 桌子
Please set up the *table* before dinnertime.

tail 〔 tel 〕 *n.* 尾巴
A monkey has a long *tail*.

Taiwan 〔ˈtaɪˈwɑn 〕 *n.* 台灣
Taiwan is a beautiful island.

take 〔 tek 〕 *v.* 拿
Mike forgot to *take* his book to school.

talk (tɔk) *v.* 談話
Andrew and Alan are *talking* on the phone.

tall (tɔl) *adj.* 高的
George is a *tall* boy.

tape (tep) *n.* 錄音帶
He recorded the speech on a *tape*.

taste (test) *v.* 嚐起來
This food *tastes* great.

taxi ('tæksɪ) *n.* 計程車
You can take a *taxi* to the airport.

tea (ti) *n.* 茶
Mother makes a pot of *tea* for us.

teach (titʃ) *v.* 教
Mr. White *teaches* English.

teacher ('titʃə) *n.* 老師
Jane's mother is a music *teacher*.

team (tim) *n.* 隊
There are eleven people on a football *team*.

teenager ('tin,edʒə) *n.* 青少年
Teenagers are boys and girls.

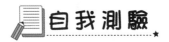

- ☐ spend   _____
- ☐ sport   _____
- ☐ stand   _____
- ☐ station   _____
- ☐ steak   _____

- ☐ store   _____
- ☐ straight   _____
- ☐ stranger   _____
- ☐ strong   _____
- ☐ successful   _____

- ☐ supermarket   _____
- ☐ swing   _____
- ☐ take   _____
- ☐ tape   _____
- ☐ team   _____

Check List

1. 蜘　蛛　　　　s ___spider___ r
2. 正方形　　　　s _____ e
3. 郵　票　　　　s _____ p
4. 開　始　　　　s _____ t
5. 胃　　　　　　s _____ h

6. 稻草；吸管　s _____ w
7. 學　習　　　　s _____ y
8. 科目；主題　s _____ t
9. 衝　浪　　　　s _____ f
10. 驚訝的　　　　s _____ d

11. 游　泳　　　　s _____ m
12. 桌　子　　　　t _____ e
13. 嚐起來　　　　t _____ e
14. 教　　　　　　t _____ h
15. 青少年　　　　t _____ r

telephone (ˈtɛləˌfon) *n.* 電話 (= *phone*)
John uses the *telephone* to talk to his friend.

television (ˈtɛləˌvɪʒən) *n.* 電視 (= *TV*)
Jack watches *television* every night.

tell (tɛl) *v.* 告訴
Please *tell* me the truth.

temple (ˈtɛmpļ) *n.* 寺廟
Many people go to the *temple* to pray.

ten (tɛn) *adj.* 十個
There are *ten* fingers on our hands.

tennis (ˈtɛnɪs) *n.* 網球
Mark is learning to play *tennis*.

terrible (ˈtɛrəbļ) *adj.* 可怕的
Last night, the storm was *terrible*.

tenth (tɛnθ) *adj.* 第十的
The *tenth* month of the year is October.

test (tɛst) *n.* 測驗
We took our English *test* this morning.

than (ðæn) *conj.* 比
Sam is taller *than* Paul.

thank 〔θæŋk〕 *v.* 感謝
The teacher *thanked* us for giving her some flowers.

that 〔ðæt〕 *adj.* 那個
I would like to take *that* book.

the 〔ðə〕 *art.* 那個
I'm going to *the* post office.

theater 〔'θiətɚ〕 *n.* 戲院
We went to the *theater* last night to watch a play.

their 〔ðɛr〕 *adj.* 他們的
The children like *their* teacher.

theirs 〔ðɛrz〕 *pron.* 他們的【they 的所有格代名詞】
These pictures are *theirs*.

them 〔ðɛm〕 *pron.* 他們【they 的受格】
The customers gave *them* a tip.

themselves 〔ðɛm'sɛlvz〕 *pron.* 他們自己【they 的反身代名詞】
Kids can't take care of *themselves*.

then 〔ðɛn〕 *adv.* 然後
Close your books and *then* put them away.

there 〔 ðɛr 〕 *adv.* 那裡
There are two apples on the table.

these 〔 ðiz 〕 *adj.* 這些
These books were kept in my room.

they 〔 ðe 〕 *pron.* 他們
They're ready to go to the party.

thick 〔 θɪk 〕 *adj.* 厚的
This is a *thick* book.

thin 〔 θɪn 〕 *adj.* 瘦的；薄的
The poor children are *thin*.

thing 〔 θɪŋ 〕 *n.* 事情；東西
There are many *things* to remember.

think 〔 θɪŋk 〕 *v.* 想；認為
I *think* she will come here today.

third 〔 θɝd 〕 *adj.* 第三的
It's the *third* time that he has come to Japan.

thirsty 〔'θɝstɪ 〕 *adj.* 口渴的
The baby is *thirsty*.

thirteen 〔 θɝ'tin 〕 *adj.* 十三的
My cousin is *thirteen*.

thirty ﹝'θɜtɪ﹞ *adj.* 三十的
My aunt is *thirty* years old.

this ﹝ðɪs﹞ *adj.* 這個
This book is not mine.

those ﹝ðoz﹞ *adj.* 那些
Those cars are old.

though ﹝ðo﹞ *conj.* 雖然 (= *although*)
Though he doesn't love me, I still love him.

thousand ﹝'θauznd﹞ *n.* 千
This watch costs one *thousand* dollars.

three ﹝θri﹞ *adj.* 三個
Sandra and Frank have *three* kids.

throat ﹝θrot﹞ *n.* 喉嚨
When we eat, food passes down our *throat*.

throw ﹝θro﹞ *v.* 丟
Richard *throws* small pieces of stone in a river.

Thursday ﹝'θɜzde﹞ *n.* 星期四
My daughter was born on *Thursday*.

ticket ﹝'tɪkɪt﹞ *n.* 票
Tom made a reservation for movie *tickets*.

tidy ('taɪdɪ) *adj.* 整齊的
Mike's room is very *tidy*.

tie (taɪ) *v.* 綁；打（結）　　*n.* 領帶
I *tied* a bow for my younger sister.

tiger ('taɪgə) *n.* 老虎
A *tiger* is a large animal that lives in the jungle.

time (taɪm) *n.* 時間
It's *time* for dinner.

tired (taɪrd) *adj.* 疲倦的
I'm *tired* from work.

to (tu) *prep.* 到…
Jim goes *to* school in the morning.

toast (tost) *n.* 吐司；敬酒；乾杯
Let's make a *toast*!

today (tə'de) *n.* 今天
Today is Nancy's birthday.

toe (to) *n.* 腳趾
I dropped a book on my big *toe*.

together (tə'gɛðə) *adv.* 一起
We can go to the store *together*.

tomato〔 təˈmeto 〕 *n.* 蕃茄
Tomatoes are used for making ketchup.

tomorrow〔 təˈmɑro 〕 *n.* 明天
Tomorrow is the day that comes after today.

tonight〔 təˈnaɪt 〕 *adv.* 今晚
Let's go to see a movie *tonight*.

too〔 tu 〕 *adv.* 太；也
The elephant is *too* big to be kept as a pet.

tool〔 tul 〕 *n.* 工具
Mechanics use a variety of *tools*.

tooth〔 tuθ 〕 *n.* 牙齒【複數是 teeth〔 tiθ 〕】
We must brush our *teeth* every morning and
night.

top〔 tɑp 〕 *n.* 頂端
He climbed to the *top* of the tree.

total〔ˈtotl̩ 〕 *adj.* 全部的；總計的
What is the *total* cost of the purchase?

touch〔 tʌtʃ 〕 *v.* 觸摸
Please don't *touch* any paintings.

towel〔ˈtauəl 〕 *n.* 毛巾
Nick carries a *towel* to the beach.

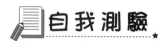

自我測驗

- ☐ telephone _____
- ☐ temple _____
- ☐ terrible _____
- ☐ theater _____
- ☐ thick _____

- ☐ thing _____
- ☐ though _____
- ☐ throat _____
- ☐ ticket _____
- ☐ tie _____

- ☐ tired _____
- ☐ toast _____
- ☐ together _____
- ☐ tomato _____
- ☐ total _____

Check List

1. 電　視　　t _____television_____ n
2. 網　球　　t _____ s
3. 測　驗　　t _____ t
4. 感　謝　　t _____ k
5. 瘦　的　　t _____ n
6. 想　　　　t _____ k
7. 口渴的　　t _____ y
8. 丟　　　　t _____ w
9. 星期四　　T _____ y
10. 整齊的　　t _____ y
11. 腳　趾　　t _____ e
12. 工　具　　t _____ l
13. 頂　端　　t _____ p
14. 觸　摸　　t _____ h
15. 毛　巾　　t _____ l

town ﹝ taʊn ﹞ *n.* 城鎮
He lives in a small *town*.

toy ﹝ tɔɪ ﹞ *n.* 玩具
Children like to play with *toys*.

traffic ﹝'træfɪk ﹞ *n.* 交通
The *traffic* is very heavy today.

train ﹝ tren ﹞ *n.* 火車
The *train* arrived on time.

trash ﹝ træʃ ﹞ *n.* 垃圾
There are few *trash* cans on the street.

treat ﹝ trit ﹞ *v.* 對待；治療；認為 *n.* 請客
I don't like the way he *treats* me.

tree ﹝ tri ﹞ *n.* 樹
There is an apple *tree* in my garden.

trick ﹝ trɪk ﹞ *n.* 詭計；把戲
I'm teaching my dog *tricks*.

trip ﹝ trɪp ﹞ *n.* 旅行
We went on a *trip* to Bali last week.

trouble ﹝'trʌbl̩ ﹞ *n.* 麻煩
It will be no *trouble* to drive you to the station.

truck ﹙ trʌk ﹚ *n.* 卡車
They hired a *truck* to move their furniture.

true ﹙ tru ﹚ *adj.* 真正的
A *true* friend will always help you.

try ﹙ traɪ ﹚ *v.* 嘗試
I'll *try* to learn French.

T-shirt (ˈtiˌʃɜt ﹚ *n.* T 恤
What kind of *T-shirt* do you wear?

tub ﹙ tʌb ﹚ *n.* 浴缸 (= *bathtub*)
Peter is cleaning the *tub*.

Tuesday (ˈtjuzde ﹚ *n.* 星期二
Tuesday is the day before Wednesday.

turkey (ˈtɜkɪ ﹚ *n.* 火雞
We had *turkey* for dinner.

turn ﹙ tɜn ﹚ *v.* 轉向；變成
Go down the street and *turn* right.

turtle (ˈtɜtl̩ ﹚ *n.* 海龜
My younger brother has two *turtles*.

twelve ﹙ twɛlv ﹚ *n.* 十二
One dozen equals *twelve*.

twenty ﹝'twɛntɪ﹞ *adj.* 二十的
It took us *twenty* minutes to get to the station.

twice ﹝twaɪs﹞ *adv.* 兩次
I rewrote the essay *twice*.

two ﹝tu﹞ *adj.* 兩個
A bicycle has *two* wheels.

type ﹝taɪp﹞ *n.* 類型　*v.* 打字
I don't like people of that *type*.

typhoon ﹝taɪ'fun﹞ *n.* 颱風
There were five *typhoons* this year.

U u

umbrella ﹝ʌm'brɛlə﹞ *n.* 雨傘
We use *umbrellas* when it rains.

uncle ﹝'ʌŋkḷ﹞ *n.* 叔叔
Paul has only one *uncle*.

under ﹝'ʌndɚ﹞ *prep.* 在…之下
A cat is sleeping *under* the tree.

understand ﹝ˌʌndɚ'stænd﹞ *v.* 了解
Peter doesn't *understand* the words.

unhappy〔ʌn'hæpɪ〕*adj.* 不快樂的

She is such an *unhappy* person.

uniform〔'junəˌfɔrm〕*n.* 制服

Many students in Taiwan have to wear *uniforms*.

until〔ən'tɪl〕*prep.* 直到

She worked there *until* last month.

up〔ʌp〕*adv.* 往上

We must stand *up* when the teacher comes in.

U.S.A. *n.* 美國 (= *United States of America*)

My brother went to the *U.S.A.* to learn English.

us〔ʌs〕*pron.* 我們【we 的受格】

They met *us* at the station.

use〔juz〕*v.* 使用

We *use* money to buy things.

useful〔'jusfəl〕*adj.* 有用的

A flashlight can be *useful* in the dark.

usually〔'juʒʊəlɪ〕*adv.* 通常

Mom *usually* leaves home at 6:30 in the morning.

V v

vacation ﹝ ve'keʃən ﹞ *n.* 假期

They were on summer *vacation*.

vegetable ﹝'vɛdʒətəbḷ﹞ *n.* 蔬菜

Rabbits mainly eat *vegetables*.

very ﹝'vɛrɪ﹞ *adv.* 非常地

The trees in the jungle are *very* tall.

vest ﹝ vɛst ﹞ *n.* 背心

I need to buy new *vests*.

video ﹝'vɪdɪ‚o﹞ *n.* 錄影帶

Videos are not popular anymore.

violin ﹝‚vaɪə'lɪn﹞ *n.* 小提琴

A *violin* is smaller than a viola.

visit ﹝'vɪzɪt﹞ *v.* 探望；參觀

We will *visit* my grandmother in Tainan.

voice ﹝ vɔɪs ﹞ *n.* 聲音

That man has a loud *voice*.

W w

wait 〔 wet 〕 *v.* 等待
Can you *wait* for me?

waiter 〔'wetɚ〕 *n.* 服務生
Alan's brother is a *waiter*.

waitress 〔'wetrɪs〕 *n.* 女服務生
The *waitress* in this restaurant is very nice.

wake 〔 wek 〕 *v.* 醒來
Jane *wakes* up at 6:00 every morning.

walk 〔 wɔk 〕 *v.* 走路
You can *walk* to the store in five minutes.

wall 〔 wɔl 〕 *n.* 牆壁
The robber climbed over the *wall* to get away.

wallet 〔'wɑlɪt〕 *n.* 皮夾
John carries his money in a *wallet*.

want 〔 wɑnt 〕 *v.* 想要
Anne *wants* a cold drink.

warm 〔 wɔrm 〕 *adj.* 溫暖的
Keep yourself *warm* in the winter.

自我測驗

- [ ] toy   _____
- [ ] train   _____
- [ ] treat   _____
- [ ] trick   _____
- [ ] true   _____

- [ ] turkey   _____
- [ ] type   _____
- [ ] umbrella   _____
- [ ] unhappy   _____
- [ ] until   _____

- [ ] vegetable   _____
- [ ] vest   _____
- [ ] visit   _____
- [ ] wait   _____
- [ ] want   _____

Check List

1.	交　通	t _____*traffic*_____	c
2.	麻　煩	t _____	e
3.	嘗　試	t _____	y
4.	轉　向	t _____	n
5.	颱　風	t _____	n
6.	了　解	u _____	d
7.	有用的	u _____	l
8.	通　常	u _____	y
9.	假　期	v _____	n
10.	錄影帶	v _____	o
11.	小提琴	v _____	n
12.	聲　音	v _____	e
13.	服務生	w _____	r
14.	醒　來	w _____	e
15.	溫暖的	w _____	m

wash〔waʃ〕*v.* 洗

We must *wash* our hands before eating meals.

watch〔watʃ〕*v.* 觀賞   *n.* 錶

Mandy likes to *watch* cartoons.

water〔'watɚ〕*n.* 水

I want to drink a glass of cold *water*.

watermelon〔'watɚˏmɛlən〕*n.* 西瓜

Do you want to have some *watermelon*?

wave〔wev〕*n.* 波浪   *v.* 揮動

The *waves* are very high today.

way〔we〕*n.* 路

Can you tell me the *way* to the station?

we〔wi〕*pron.* 我們

We will go to the movies this weekend.

weak〔wik〕*adj.* 虛弱的

My grandfather is very *weak*.

wear〔wɛr〕*v.* 穿

She is *wearing* a new dress.

weather〔'wɛðɚ〕*n.* 天氣

The *weather* is good here.

Wednesday (ˈwɛnzde) *n.* 星期三
Wednesday is the day after Tuesday.

week (wik) *n.* 星期
There are seven days in a *week*.

weekend (ˈwikˈɛnd) *n.* 週末
What are you going to do this *weekend*?

welcome (ˈwɛlkəm) *v.* 歡迎
We always *welcome* guests to our restaurant.

well (wɛl) *adv.* 很好地
She speaks English and Japanese *well*.

west (wɛst) *n.* 西方
The sun sets in the *west*.

wet (wɛt) *adj.* 濕的
Be careful of the *wet* floor.

whale (hwel) *n.* 鯨
A *whale* is the biggest animal living in the sea.

what (hwɑt) *pron.* 什麼
I didn't know *what* you meant.

when (hwɛn) *adv.* 何時
When did John visit the zoo?

where ﹙hwɛr﹚ *adv.* 哪裡
Where do you live?

whether ﹙'hwɛðɚ﹚ *conj.* 是否
I'm not sure *whether* it will rain.

which ﹙hwɪtʃ﹚ *pron.* 哪一個
Which of the two were you talking about?

white ﹙hwaɪt﹚ *adj.* 白色的
When people grow old, their hair turns *white*.

who ﹙hu﹚ *pron.* 誰
Who is the new boy in the class?

whose ﹙huz﹚ *adj.* 誰的
Whose shoes are those?

why ﹙hwaɪ﹚ *adv.* 為什麼
Why did she run away from home?

wife ﹙waɪf﹚ *n.* 妻子
His *wife* is a nurse.

will ﹙wɪl﹚ *aux.* 將
Cathy *will* play golf on Sunday.

win ﹙wɪn﹚ *v.* 贏
Rose will do anything to *win* the game.

wind 〔 wɪnd 〕 *n.* 風
The great *wind* blew across the sea.

window 〔 'wɪndo 〕 *n.* 窗戶
A car has four *windows*.

windy 〔 'wɪndɪ 〕 *adj.* 多風的
It's *windy* today.

winter 〔 'wɪntɚ 〕 *n.* 冬天
Winter is the season that comes after autumn.

wise 〔 waɪz 〕 *adj.* 有智慧的
My grandfather is a *wise* old man.

wish 〔 wɪʃ 〕 *v.* 希望
What do you *wish* to have for Christmas?

with 〔 wɪθ 〕 *prep.* 用；有
Peter writes *with* his left hand.

without 〔 wɪð'aʊt 〕 *prep.* 沒有
We can't live *without* water.

woman 〔 'wʊmən 〕 *n.* 女人
The *woman* with long hair is Tom's mother.

wonderful 〔 'wʌndɚfəl 〕 *adj.* 很棒的
Ida and I had a *wonderful* time.

word 〔 wɝd 〕 *n.* 字
You can look up the new *words* in the dictionary.

work 〔 wɝk 〕 *v.* 工作
Rebecca *works* in a bank.

workbook 〔'wɝk,bʊk 〕 *n.* 工作手冊；作業簿
My boss asked us to read the *workbook* carefully.

worker 〔'wɝkɚ 〕 *n.* 工人
His father is a *worker*.

world 〔 wɝld 〕 *n.* 世界
Mt. Everest is the tallest mountain in the *world*.

worry 〔'wɝɪ 〕 *v.* 擔心
Don't *worry* about me.

would 〔 wʊd 〕 *aux.* 將【will 的過去式】
Would you like a cup of coffee?

write 〔 raɪt 〕 *v.* 寫
We *write* with pens or pencils.

writer 〔'raɪtɚ 〕 *n.* 作家
A *writer* is someone who writes books.

wrong 〔 rɔŋ 〕 *adj.* 錯誤的
My answer was *wrong*, so I erased it.

Y y

yard 〔 jɑrd 〕 *n.* 院子
Children are playing in the front *yard*.

yeah 〔 jɛ 〕 *adv.* 是的 (= *yes*)
Yeah, I see.

year 〔 jɪr 〕 *n.* 年
A new *year* begins on January 1st.

yellow 〔 'jɛlo 〕 *adj.* 黃色的
Shirley likes to wear her *yellow* dress.

yes 〔 jɛs 〕 *adv.* 是的
"Is it raining?" "*Yes*, it is."

yesterday 〔 'jɛstɚde 〕 *n.* 昨天
It was raining *yesterday*.

yet 〔 jɛt 〕 *adv.* 還 (沒)
The work is not *yet* finished.

you 〔 ju 〕 *pron.* 你
The teacher wants to see *you* for a moment.

young 〔 jʌŋ 〕 *adj.* 年輕的
Lucy is too *young* to have a baby.

your 〔 jʊr 〕 *adj.* 你的【you 的所有格】
I'm glad to be *your* friend.

yours 〔 jʊrz 〕 *pron.* 你的【you 的所有格代名詞】
This book is *yours*.

yourself 〔 jʊr'sɛlf 〕 *pron.* 你自己【you 的反身
代名詞】
Please take care of *yourself*.

yourselves 〔 jʊr'sɛlvz 〕 *pron.* 你們自己
【you 的反身代名詞】
You are keeping *yourselves* busy.

yummy 〔'jʌmɪ 〕 *adj.* 好吃的
How *yummy* that cake was!

Z z

zebra 〔'zibrə 〕 *n.* 斑馬
A *zebra* has black and white stripes all over its body.

zero 〔'zɪro 〕 *n.* 零
The last digit of her telephone number is *zero*.

zoo 〔 zu 〕 *n.* 動物園
There are many kinds of animals in the *zoo*.

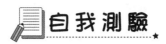
自我測驗

- [ ] watch   _____
- [ ] wave   _____
- [ ] weak   _____
- [ ] wet   _____
- [ ] whale   _____

- [ ] wife   _____
- [ ] wind   _____
- [ ] wise   _____
- [ ] work   _____
- [ ] worry   _____

- [ ] wrong   _____
- [ ] yard   _____
- [ ] young   _____
- [ ] yummy   _____
- [ ] zoo   _____

Check List

1. 洗　　　　w _____ *wash* _____ h
2. 穿　　　　w _____ r
3. 天　氣　　w _____ r
4. 週　末　　w _____ d
5. 歡　迎　　w _____ e

6. 贏　　　　w _____ n
7. 窗　戶　　w _____ w
8. 希　望　　w _____ h
9. 很棒的　　w _____ l
10. 世　界　　w _____ d

11. 寫　　　　w _____ e
12. 作　家　　w _____ r
13. 黃色的　　y _____ w
14. 昨　天　　y _____ y
15. 斑　馬　　z _____ a

跟著百萬網紅「單詞教父劉毅」學英文

　　你在捷運上，看到的都是手機。用手機聊天、玩遊戲、都是浪費時間，用手機上「快手」、「抖音」網站，用英文留言，這是心對心的交流，朋友越多，英文越進步。

　　每堂課平均約30秒，每天有2~3堂課，任何時間、任何地點都可以重複練習，在線上從小學、國中、高中、大學到成人，不分年齡、不分程度，人人可學可和劉毅老師一對一討論，什麼問題都可以問，有問必答！用劉毅老師說的話來留言，寫得愈多，進步愈多！可以輕鬆應付任何考試！

→ 立即掃描QR碼，下載「快手」、「抖音」，搜尋「單詞教父劉毅」，
　點讚、分享及關注，成為粉絲，享受免費英語課程！

國中會考必備 1200 字【創新錄音版】
1200 Fundamental Vocabulary
for Junior High School Students

附錄音 QR 碼 售價：150 元

主　　　編 / 劉　毅

發　行　所 / 學習出版有限公司

　　　　　　TEL (02) 2704-5525

郵 撥 帳 號 / 05127272 學習出版社帳戶

登 記 證 / 局版台業 2179 號

印　刷　所 / 裕強彩色印刷有限公司

台 北 門 市 / 台北市許昌街 17 號 6F

　　　　　　TEL (02) 2331-4060

台灣總經銷 / 紅螞蟻圖書有限公司

　　　　　　TEL (02) 2795-3656

本公司網址 / www.learnbook.com.tw

電 子 郵 件 / learnbook0928@gmail.com

2023 年 8 月 1 日二版一刷

ISBN 978-986-231-482-1